to a true educate love ~j . (handwritten inscription)

Dreaming the Impossible to Build the Extraordinary

The Formative First Year of Architectural Education
Frosso Pimenides with Jeremy Melvin

The Bartlett
School of
Architecture

UCL

THE BARTLETT

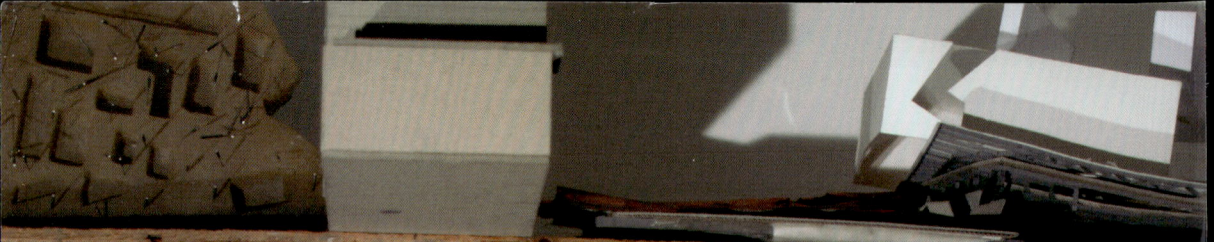

0.1

Contents

0.2

NAVALIS

Foreword: Pimenides and Pedagogy

Professor Alan Penn

In 2018, I visited Venice for the architecture biennale. It has become
something of a tradition for my wife Alison and I, as I suspect it has for many
others. It is of course not only about the biennale, but also the city itself:
its churches and art, *palazzi* and *scuole*, the *campi* with their wellheads, the
light polarised by the water and subtly filtered by the haze of the humid heat,
the canals and *vaporetti*, and the welcome absence of cars, which makes the
acoustics all the more perceptible. You hear the murmur of voices and flutter
of footsteps before you see people, or you never see them at all, the sound
reflecting off walls around narrow chicanes in passageways or coming from
upper windows. The sculpted stone and damp smell of crumbling plaster
walls, stripped to reveal ruddy brick and white lime mortar, bear witness to
past splendour and a pride that seeks to retain rather than renew historic
fabric. The unlikeliness of the site – the seeming impossibility of constructing
anything permanent on the constantly shifting mud flats and sand banks of
the lagoon; knowing that everything sits on wooden piles from the Republic's
alpine forests, centuries old, but which somehow fail to rot when all else
seems to crumble – lends an air of the surreal. The history of the Republic of
Venice, which reached its peak over 500 years ago, ruling over and trading
with much of the Mediterranean, dictating law and military might, conserving
crafts and creating institutions, pervades the city.

In amongst this, on the streets and canals but mainly in the bars,
are groups of architects from all over the globe, distinctive in their guild
regalia of crushed black and grey linen, statement spectacles and geodesic
jewellery. Come together, like some totemic society on the biennial
pilgrimage to the *vernissage*, they exchange gossip and retell creation
myths for a new generation. The Republic is not dead, just reconstituted
as a global phenomenon in solidarity for art, dance, drama, cinema, music
and architecture. The biennales are on a regular cycle, drawing crowds and
sending them back around the world, newly reconnected to their global
communities of practice.

This is the product of architectural education: the creation of a community, with all the accoutrements of norms and values, codes of practice and dress, working methods and assumptions, overt behaviours and esoterica, and above all a set of ways of seeing the world.

In this book, Frosso Pimenides and Jeremy Melvin describe how this alchemical process of social transmutation begins. It is uncodified in the main, for very good reason. If it were easy, we would be surrounded by wonderful architecture; we are not. There are occasional gems and then there is a much more pervasive substrate of humdrum building. This is the product of many architects and non-architects working in practices and for clients who really do not understand or necessarily care what architecture is.

What architecture is and is not

A spider conducts operations that resemble those of a weaver, and a bee puts to shame many an architect in the construction of her cells. But what distinguishes the worst architect from the best of bees is this, that the architect raises his structure in imagination before he erects it in reality. At the end of every labour-process, we get a result that already existed in the imagination of the labourer at its commencement.[1]

Architects envision what the world might be. Let us be clear by contrasting a pair of stereotypes; invoking stereotypes is just a device to make a point, we do not imply that they are real. We propose that the properties of each of these represent the ends of an axis, but these ends do not map onto specific professional titles implied by the stereotype. Consider the stereotypical engineer. They have been educated in the laws of physics and trained to use these to model how a system will perform. The laws of physics are based on empirical observations. We project forward from these to model something as-yet unbuilt. In the world of physical behaviour – of structure, light and sound, for example – this works well, until it does not, and then we learn from our mistakes and engineering progresses. For example, the design of bridges has progressed through a series of failures: Tacoma Narrows (1940) failed through resonance in wind; the West Gate Bridge (1970), through flange failure; and the Millennium Bridge (2000) through coupling of human gait and sideways motion.[2]

1. Karl Marx, *Capital: A Critique of Political Economy*, vol. 1, Penguin, 1980, p. 284.
2. Tacoma Narrows Bridge, Puget Sound, Washington State, US, completed and failed in 1940; West Gate Bridge, Melbourne, Australia, failed during construction in 1970; Millennium Bridge, London, UK, completed and wobbled in 2000.

At each stage, the assumptions of the past have proven inadequate to predict new kinds of failure developed through innovation and increases in scale. In each case new codes are added to the engineering design manual and progress takes place. This mode of practice clearly demonstrates learning and applies it to reduce risk of failure. The stereotypical engineer asks for a clear statement of design objectives, and then reviews the repertoire of solution strategies and models the implications of each for attaining those objectives. The process is essentially linear, projecting forward from known cases in the past to model new designs. The failures described above each occurred when the design evolved to the point that previous satisfactory conditions no longer held true. West Gate Bridge's box girder was increased in scale to the point where catastrophic flange buckling occurred. With the benefit of hindsight, many of these failures seem predictable – and indeed they are when you know to look – but at the time they were not. The basis of engineering practice lies in empirical science and precedent case history. This has a strong effect towards specialisation within the discipline and is characterised in terms of bodies of specialist knowledge.

Next, let us look at an equally stereotypical architect. Here, the basis of practice lies somewhere very different. Stereotypically, architecture does not predict on the basis of the past, but envisions a future and then works to conjure it up. Rather than specialising in specific aspects of physical function, architects must synthesise across functional domains – heat, light, sound, smell, structure, material, human behaviour and emotion – to construct the environments we inhabit and find meaningful. Architecture's primary purposes, however, are most often social or subjective, with the physical creating the conditions for these. What this means is that people, their interactions, responses and behaviours, form the centre of architecture. Although this does not rule out empirical knowledge from an architectural process, it does add considerably to the complexity involved in gaining that knowledge.

Many of these factors can be considered as systems in their own right. Often these systems are essentially independent, but they can interact in complex ways. For example, a building's structure functions according to the laws of structural engineering but it also has thermal mass, which affects environmental performance. This behaviour is further complicated by the way that people interact with the building: a building in a hot climate will perform quite differently if the inhabitants do not understand the principles at play and open windows during the heat of the day. If you open the windows at night, allowing air to cool the high thermal-mass structure, and then close them during the day, the building will retain the cool temperature. In this way, culturally learned human behaviours can interact with physical fabric to affect environmental performance. This is particularly important since physics alone has proven a poor predictor of performance given the interaction of buildings with their users.

The point of this kind of complex interactive system is that making predictions based on empirical experience can be of limited value. Instead, what architects do is design for a future that may never have existed before. The pressure here is to innovate and to provide a vision that then leads the project team through a design process. These kinds of complexity have led to training architects in the use of intuition to synthesise numerous independent but interacting systems, and this is probably the primary method in practice.

Architectural practices seem to come from a single culture and seek to differentiate themselves as much as possible within that culture, in terms of what they produce and how they set about doing it. This force to differentiate seems to form an underlying motivation amongst practice, insofar as any is discernible. For example, practices differentiate themselves in terms of stylistic, aesthetic, spatial, and formal properties of their architecture, and in terms of the working processes they adopt to develop a design. Some adopt a highly rational approach, others a more arts-based practice; and they differentiate themselves in terms of the values and ideological positions they espouse, some driven by a community or sustainability ideology, others by a more commercial set of values.

One way to think of this is in terms of how the practice of architecture as a whole offers the client choice. One of the first decisions a client must make is to choose their architect. Some will do so on the basis of the architect's previous work and what this looks like, others will prefer to choose an architect whose approach to design seems sympathetic to the client or their organisation or on the basis of shared values or ideology, and most on some combination of all of these. There is, therefore, a pressure for different practices to differentiate themselves in terms of their offer to prospective clients. At the same time, however, the industry is subject to fashions and trends, as are clients. A building 'says' something about those that commission it, and this statement can be radical or conservative. The profession as a whole must offer clients a choice in this and so there is a pressure to differentiate as much as possible. At the same time, any architect who specialises so much that the number of clients becomes too small will not last long or build much.

There is a role in this social milieu for the architectural writer, critic and historian. By surveying architectural practice, searching for patterns and then translating these into language, the critic helps practice to be reflective and moves products of intuition into the realm of discussion and debate. This in turn shapes the lens through which practitioners see their own work and that of others, and helps them define their own pathways. This might be by emulation of ideas they appreciate or by focussing on those they wish to distinguish themselves from. Taken together, these provide the main dynamics through which architectural culture evolves.

Flocking architects

Craig Reynolds' Boids (1987) simulation of flocking birds was based on a very simple rule-set. Boids fly on a trajectory defined by the average of the trajectories of other boids in their immediate surroundings.[3] The astonishing thing he showed was that this simple rule emulated the remarkable natural phenomenon of a murmuration of starlings, where the flock appears to exist as a single object. Truly one of the natural world's greatest shows of aerial ballet, the murmuration flows, twists and turns above the landscape, at times dividing and then coalescing, stretching and condensing. It is hard to believe that the birds, in their thousands, do this for any other reason than an aesthetic delight in collaborative creativity. As individual architects define their practice, they move through the space of design possibilities. On occasion they see the work of other practitioners and draw inspiration from that; on occasion, through critical practice, they seek to distinguish their approach from that of others or the current fashion. Like Reynolds' boids, they flock together and diverge. The vast body of practitioners follow the common trajectory, but those at the leading edge continually shape their own paths to explore new territory. These are the 'star architects' whose work shapes the contemporary debate. On occasion the flock may divide, as radically differing approaches emerge that split practice into distinct groups. Over time these may merge again, or disappear, as a once-promising seam is found to be blind.

Imagine that the whole community of architectural practice is exploring possible new forms of society and the spaces that these inhabit. That exploration is informed by contemporary society and current concerns, as well as by visionary and fictional arts and culture, and by the new technologies that affect how society is created and how the environments

---

3. Craig Reynolds, 'Flocks, Herds and Schools: A Distributed Behavioral Model', *ACM SIGGRAPH Computer Graphics*, vol. 21, no. 4, 1987, pp. 25–34

we build are delivered and operate. There are no limits to architectural concerns and so the space of possibility is infinite, limited only by the architect's imagination and perceptions of risk.

Since, as Karl Marx had it, the 'architect raises his structure in imagination before he erects it in reality',[4] the exploration of the infinite space of possibility is mainly a theoretical project. We test our theories by building them. Some succeed, or even exceed, our expectations. Others are resounding failures. Unlike engineers, however, who have a means of learning from experience because expected performance is codified in the laws of physics and engineering models, architects often repeat the mistakes of the past.

Although in architecture bad ideas often seem to stick, there is a saving grace: those bad ideas, once built, become a part of the context for further design and create opportunities to be exploited. Bad ideas have a habit of not realising their full value and, of course, this is inherently valuable: it creates space at a lower rent that is available for genuine innovation and new market entrants. In a city, these edge spaces are often the most vibrant. The innovators appropriate the affordances of the structure for new uses: car parks become cinemas or arts venues, and leftover spaces become street markets.

This is the context for architectural education, which is less defined by a body of knowledge to be transferred and more by a mode of practice. Architectural knowledge is, if anything, embodied; and architectural education is a process of training, exercise and rehearsal in a cerebral and physical dance.

Trust and transformation

Trust lies at the heart of performance: trust in oneself and in others. There are fundamental moves, reactions and responses that must become second nature if an architect is to perform as part of a group in collaborative creativity. Trust in oneself is displayed as confidence. However, when misplaced, this trust merely displays arrogance; there is a fine line between the two. Understanding this line and becoming self-aware enough to appreciate when one is stepping over it is a part of architectural education.

4. Marx, *Capital*, 1980, p. 284.

Building trust in and amongst others is a different kind of task, but both confidence and humility are important components. It seems easier for those that are confident in their own abilities to collaborate, but equally those that are aware of their own limitations seem better able to listen and to take advice.

To build self-confidence while also building self-critical awareness and humility is hard, but this is a primary task of architectural education. It requires one to learn to switch between a consideration of the individual and of individuals' relationships to one another; to understand that the individual is constructed as much by their personal characteristics as by the social context of their membership of the collective; and to understand that they are as much a product of what they know as what they do not know. Having two ways of looking at a system at the same time is fundamentally architectural in nature, with the key skill being to flip one's perception between perspectives.

Fragments and wholes

The idea of there being two ways of looking applies as much to the physical and spatial world that we design, construct and inhabit as it does to the individuals and groups that do the designing. The world is composed of fragments that come together to make a whole. Architecture is exactly a 'part-whole' system. Considering fragments and how they come together to make a whole is perhaps the architect's main concern. It is the concern of construction but also of the way that architecture becomes meaningful to people. We see just part at any instant from any viewpoint, but over time we construct in our minds an understanding of the way that parts relate to create a whole. In this sense, architecture transcends both space and time, looking at once from multiple points of view and compiling our experience from instants over time. This is how meaning is constructed from the most prosaic of experiences and episodes to create an understanding of how we relate to the world.

By studying fragments and collections of fragments, the student confronts the possible logical relations from which meaning is composed. The system is open – there is no predefined right answer – and this leads to learning about how to consider the openness of part-whole relationships.

Places as parts in context

Places can also be thought of in terms of fragments and wholes, but in this case the fragments are predominantly spaces. Places are composed of the way systems of spaces come together, while spaces are formed by the way that buildings come together. The spaces and the buildings are used by people, and this life animates and makes the place social. It is this complex and multi-layered set of relations in space that the notion of 'place' must capture.

To ask a student in their first year to comprehend this directly might seem unfair, and so the approach is to ask them to intervene in a real context by designing and constructing an installation. By making an intervention, the complexity of real-world conditions cannot be ignored. Working at the scale of real space and through intervention means it is essential that students work in groups, thus requiring them to develop trusted relationships.

Teaching Architecture is keeping one's feet on the ground and one's head amongst the clouds; it is to dream the extraordinary, and to build the impossible.

In a community of students where each and every member is unique, it is important to encourage them to be naughty as well as serious, to care for each other, celebrate mistakes, to turn disasters upside down, and learn to never give up.

It is not only the magic of witnessing a young person turn into an imaginative thinker and designer, but it is also the daily struggles between the mundane and the sublime, the disastrous and the triumphant, the laughing and the crying that stay with us over the years!

All those students, colleagues, teachers, mentors, family and friends who over the years have given us the motivation, strength and support to question what architectural education is all about? I want to thank them all for their dedication to our common cause of believing that through architectural ideas, one can change the world.

Frosso Pimenides, RIBA Fellowship Acceptance Speech,
2 February 2015, Jarvis Hall, RIBA

0.3

Preface

Professor Frosso Pimenides

This book is a reflection on my life at The Bartlett as a Director of the Architecture BSc Year 1 since 1990. It is a collection of my thoughts and practices relating to the overarching question I have had in mind over my 30 years at the school: How do you initiate someone into architectural education? The gut reaction to this always seems to come back to people, places and objects, and the myriad stories that connect them.

This book presents a long and ongoing engagement with architectural education that is quite specific to the first year. It should not be taken as a set of fixed instructions but more as a set of attitudes and approaches. Every person is unique and every situation or site is particular. These methods are the result of many years of first-hand observation, study, practice, teaching, connecting with people, travelling, living, thinking, doing, and asking the difficult questions about our role and the road into the future of architectural learning and practice.

The magic of the unknown

I often wonder how someone can do the same job for so many years and manage to not get bored or repeat oneself, but to strive ultimately to improve what we are doing. If we have the feeling that each year is a fresh start, it is because we are faced with the magic of the unknown: every year we have around 100 new students, and we always have new themes and project regions. It is these unknown ingredients and qualities that keep us going; the motivation and enthusiasm comes from the minds and personalities that we interact with. The more experienced we become as teachers and architects, the more we enjoy not knowing and teaching students to love the freshness and magic of the unknown. Successful moments often seem to come when we embrace this. There is also a fine balance between flux and the gradually accumulated stability of a group of colleagues, teachers and designers, including my co-directors, coming and going over 30 years, who have formed our teaching team. In a way, my role has been to keep some continuity amidst these shifts.

Our mission as teachers, in introducing students to the magic of architecture and higher education, is not to deliver an objective or universal recipe of how one acquires the knowledge and skills to succeed. It is to welcome this cohort of fresh minds and gradually uncover and discover their personalities, strengths and fragilities, and the insights and values of their individual cultures. It is often a process of evoking surprise, encouraging new creativity to surface after the sometimes restricting effects of secondary education. Conventions they may have been conforming to need to be shaken off in ways that help students to understand their power to change the world, and their duty to make life better for themselves and others. Maybe all we need to do is help them open a door slightly and from there go out to explore the world. Rather than overload them with knowledge, we support them to learn how to express and cultivate ideas and values, and then translate these into design practice.

As first-year tutors, we listen, suggest and support. We advance design projects *with* students – as one does in practice – not leaving them unguided. We simultaneously play many academic and pastoral roles: that of teacher, design colleague, family member, advisor and, occasionally, confidante. The alchemy of tutors and students is inspirational and rewarding, as well as, at times, challenging. The transformation binds us into a closely-knit community, within which there is always a mix of characters, where everybody is unique and is encouraged to remain so whilst supporting each other. There are ups and downs, and memories stay with us over the years; they are often the foundation of lifelong friendships and enduring reflections.

At the end of each year, these strangers have gradually discovered more about who they are, what they are interested in, and above all *why* it is important to believe in the unknown they are trying to discover. When it goes well, they will have gained the confidence to express themselves graphically and produce designs that are relevant to their interests and values.

The first year of architectural education is potentially the most formative year of an architect's life. For some it is the beginning of a way of life that starts in their first year of study and ends at the end of their lives. The title of this book expresses, for me, the very essence of what we should offer as an initiation to the profession: the real need for any fresh mind to dream the extraordinary and build the impossible.

As educators, we endeavour to nurture a collective culture across a large cohort, as well as to support, nurture and enthuse the diverse personalities that constitute this group. This experience evolves at various speeds, and at later levels in the school. Between the routine and habitual, attention to special moments, events and exciting experiments is honed and trained.

In the foreword, Professor Alan Penn, dean of The Bartlett from 2009 to 2019, highlights many important points that characterise architectural education. As well as the particular habits and set of beliefs that characterise architectural culture, they include the importance of trust between staff and students, and the scope this gives to take risks. We elaborate on these ideas in the following chapters.

Why is the first year of architectural education so compelling and invigorating?

One of the great beauties of architecture is that each time, it is like life starting all over again.[5]

— The dialogue and the chance to engage with the fresh, inquisitive approach of young minds.
— The privilege of supporting young people and those new to the field to enable them to bring all their hidden talents and wild ideas to the surface.
— The quick decision-making and constant adjustments that the complexity of this operation requires.
— The two diametric scales of operation: the collective endeavour, parallel to 1:1 listening, and helping individuals to develop their own agendas.
— The transformation from starting out as strangers to gradually building up a community; a culture within which teachers and students learn in parallel.
— The annual unknowns: new students, often new tutors, new locations, new themes to be explored, and new situations to be addressed, tackled and resolved.

This book is the result of conversations between myself and the critic and curator Jeremy Melvin, which took place over two years. Our collaboration began with a series of discussions, rifling through numerous fragments of

---

5. Widely attributed to the architect Renzo Piano.

writing and imagery, stitched together here. Melvin is a Bartlett alumnus, oftentimes lecturer and now a visiting professor, and was editor of the school's 175th anniversary publication,[6] so has an overview of its history, vicissitudes and success. He has brought a wealth of insider knowledge to the conversation, but has also introduced invaluable thematic threads that have helped to structure my 30 years of experience and thought.

We consider what is important when introducing new students to architectural education. This element of the book is in part a manifesto for a particular way of teaching and sets out some of the challenges to get there. A generation ago there was more experimentation, which we believe to be vital for education, something that the educationalist Sir Ken Robinson was keen to point out. Now, education as a route to prosperity is taken for granted, and people are more averse to taking risks. Several factors have led to this, and it seems that we have to fight against some new challenges:

— Digital media has led to shortcuts in the process of producing designs. A glossy, finished product using this technology can cover up bad ideas. The medium has increasingly become the message. We need to be wary of how digital technology has changed thinking. People are increasingly impatient to succeed and love shortcuts and quick fixes.
— Individualism makes it more difficult to create collective collaboration.
— There is a rush to get a finished product. How can you experiment while managing deadlines? Are deadlines and experiments polar opposites? How can they work together?
— Communication has become increasingly distant, inevitably linked to the developments in technology for remote exchange.
— There can seem to be a lack of interest in common sense approaches and solutions.

Teachers, with their individual experiences, characters and quirks, are vital, yet many forces are shifting young students towards a production mindset, perhaps too early. Economic and time pressures create tension between teaching and practising, but there are huge benefits for students who are given the opportunity to work with professionals who are themselves occasionally practising within the teaching environment.

The first year of architectural education often lays the foundations for a lifelong love affair with the weird world of architecture. It introduces fresh

6. Jeremy Melvin and Bob Sheil, editors, *The Bartlett 175*, Architectural Review, 2016.

minds to a world in which dream and reality are always in parallel. Students enter a new way of thinking and a new way of communicating: they learn to be active citizens and to care about the planet, the city and its politics, and the environment.[7] They are initiated into the skills, tricks of the trade and ideas that we need to have as guiding principles; they start appreciating their past, learn how to look at history critically, make drawings, models, construct and dream of a whole new world. We do not aim for exquisite drawings and artefacts, but rather to use drawing and making to nurture students' creativity, so that in future years they are empowered with the confidence to deal with all sorts of unknown situations.

7. Here I use 'politics' in its fullest and original sense: the word is derived from the Greek *politēs* (citizen) and *polis* (city).

0.4

Introduction

Jeremy Melvin

This book follows the themes Frosso Pimenides identifies as the crucial elements in her teaching practice. Each of these themes has a life beyond and outside the specific contingencies of architectural education, and in particular has roots, entrails and implications in wider social and cultural conditions.

Five themed chapters follow. Each deals with an important element in Pimenides' teaching practice. The first theme we examine is 'people and networks'. This identifies not just people who have had a significant role in the emergence of Pimenides' teaching practice, but also how she has forged networks – the dynamics between people – to achieve her goal of creating a space where students can explore and develop their own ideas and identities within the context of an educational 'circle of safety'.[8] It is an obvious subject in education but is treated here in a heterogeneous fashion, looking at people who have influenced and collaborated with Pimenides, including family members, friends and colleagues; how and what she has selected from them; and how she has used their ideas and influence as part of working relationships. Trust emerges as the essential bonding agent in these relationships, reinforced by loyalty.

The first chapter also recounts the circumstances of Pimenides' arrival at The Bartlett and the background to her approach to teaching. One of the challenges in setting out her educational practice is that sorting out the staffing and agenda for the next year has always and rightly taken priority over reflection on the past, and now there is so much past that it is impossible to reconstruct a chronology of each stage in the process.

When Pimenides first accepted the invitation to take up her role, she spent much of the summer holed up in a friend's flat 'thinking out' her teaching programme. She drew together strands from earlier teaching experiences, her work as a practising architect and her interests and ideas that had been fermenting for decades. The bones of that programme are still

8. Simon Sinek, *Leaders Eat Last: Why Some Teams Pull Together and Others Don't*, Portfolio Penguin, 2014. Sinek explains how the concept – taken from Aesop – can make a disparate group of people feel confident in working together and so achieve better results, pp. 25–30.

recognisable in the tasks she sets students, from the brief to the choice of site. She describes this challenge:

Asked to rethink and lead what year-one education was about I locked myself in a friend's kitchen for three days. I was trying to remember everything I had done and everything that mattered to me. At the same time I was trying to be an ignorant child, remembering nothing and imagining what I would like to have fun with. Writing a new course content to initiate and train students for their first year of architecture was a dilemma. Would you teach them a lot of skills and risk running out of time? Or would you give them the confidence and the time to have fun, experiment, and make mistakes?

Much of Pimenides' understanding of groups and the dynamics between individuals is empirical and derived from experience. But we also seek to show how her ideas do not exist entirely within a vacuum. We show how there are echoes in the work of noted contemporary thinkers like the historian Niall Ferguson, academic Henry Louis Gates Jr., theorist and activist Jane Jacobs, and the writer and public speaker Simon Sinek. Overall, these analogies and affinities, rather than direct influences, tend to underline one of Pimenides' most important points, that architectural education has its own culture, which is itself part of a wider culture. Encouraging students to appreciate architectural culture as a stepping-stone to being able to draw on and contribute to the riches of this wider culture is one of the central aims of her teaching practice.

The chapter concludes with a section on the experience of making a show of work as the culmination of the year, where people's conventional roles are often challenged and students are encouraged to convey their transformation as thinkers. As Pimenides explains:

To understand people is the first goal of architecture. You need empathy for people. If not, how can buildings fulfil their duty to make people's lives better? Gadgets, however useful for particular tasks, can have the cumulative effect of alienating us and corrupting our ideals in making buildings. Also, there is sometimes a fear of helping students to develop their own personalities, of recognising what, in the role of a teacher, can be offered or imagined.

Pimenides encourages students to welcome people from the past or other parts of their lives, like parents and teachers, and from the present, such as fellow students and staff, into their consciousness and thought patterns, in the same way that she invites them into her own practice.

The second chapter is on places, another obvious subject, at least in an architecture school. It addresses how Pimenides came to develop a sense of place. This started with her introduction both to real places and their mythological readings in her native Greece. As a student she began to appreciate London as a source of particular places with potential for the collective experience of being sites for design projects. There is also some consideration of the sites of field trips, and for the performances and installations that form a vital part of her teaching experience. The places explored are not just the regular, everyday locations that students may encounter, the sites where their projects are located or those they visit on field trips. They include all of these, but leavened with famous sites of great importance are negligible places – spotted by Pimenides' acute eye – where momentarily something extraordinary happens. Together, what they depict is far greater than a single student project but, like the networks of people, they define a series of physical and cultural conditions within which a project can be nurtured.

The first question about places in this context is how to understand the site of a design project; only then is building possible. Sites in London, or any other city, have particular characteristics that shape both the practical constraints and the imaginative space for students' designs. Field trips to other cities play an important part in helping students to cultivate sensitivity to place, and for this reason it is vital that they both read about the destination city and experience how it is inhabited.

Following on from that, the third chapter looks at the objects and fragments that Pimenides has accumulated over 30 years, and tries to tease out their role in her teaching practice. Almost always they stand for something greater, either because they are literally fragments of a bigger piece or more often they are reminiscent of an important idea or memory, and sometimes they are simply an example of material craftsmanship. Here, too, we indicate analogies and affinities with contemporary thinkers.

Throughout her teaching career, Pimenides has collected objects of all sorts: some are made by students or colleagues, others are found on sites or are selected for a random reason, or because they are mnemonic of past experience. For Pimenides, objects are not just functional or superficially decorative. They also evoke the time and people who made them, and the connections and networks to which they belong. In a fragmentary state, they act as metonyms for the whole they once might have been or could still become. In this way they conjure up a wider culture as well as the contingencies of a specific moment. Reminiscent of the Renaissance concept of a memory theatre, these objects help to remind Pimenides who she is, prompt visitors to make their own connections, and reinforce the idea that inspiration can come from almost any source. The objects are artfully displayed in her offices, which appear at first to be arranged with utter abandon, but each represents a moment, idea or person that has had some significance. Once these are revealed, the arrangement of the objects acquires not quite a clear rationale, but a part in a network of ideas that represents studio culture, the subject of the fourth chapter.

Studio culture is more than the animating force for selecting and arranging objects: it is the culmination of the role those objects play, interacting with people and places, and so the core of what this book is about. Studio culture is both about the studio spaces themselves – how they are configured, managed and furnished to encourage certain sorts of interaction – and the underlying knowledge and beliefs that are communicated therein. Based firmly on real people, places, things and discussion, studio culture merges them all into an ethos that allows for the free exchange of ideas in a trusting and confidence-building context. It both represents architecture and draws deeply on its culture. It is this that led Níall McLaughlin, The Bartlett's professor of architectural practice, to describe Pimenides' role as 'bearing witness to what it is to be an architect'.[9]

The final chapter is on installations. Each year, groups of students have made site-specific installations in carefully selected London locations. As Pimenides explains, they document the stages of architectural thinking.

One reason why a study of Pimenides' teaching practice is timely is that this 30-year period has seen The Bartlett transform from an underperforming design school with an excellent graduate and research capability, within one of the world's leading universities, to one of the most respected schools of architecture internationally. There were harbingers of this potential in the late 1980s, but the change hinged around Peter Cook's appointment in early 1990, when he invited Pimenides to take on the first year. It was a remarkable invitation in many ways. Cook and Pimenides were aware of each other from afar, both knowing the legendary chair of the Architectural Association, Alvin Boyarsky, with whom Cook had taught for decades and who had invited Pimenides to run a unit for second- and third-year students a few years earlier, part of what was then a portfolio career that combined teaching with private practice. Boyarsky tried to persuade Pimenides not to accept Cook's offer to go to a rival school, but The Bartlett offered her a firmer base.

9. Melvin and Sheil, *The Bartlett 175*, 2016, p. 37.

It is clear that over and above personal relationships, the first year is even more crucial – or perhaps crucial in different ways – for architecture than other subjects. Before arriving at architecture school, few students have any academic or educational experience of the subject. They may have seen many buildings, sometimes in the company of knowledgeable companions; they may, often as part of art or art history courses, have encountered historic architecture; they may have gained work experience in architects' offices. They may even have tried their hand at designing or drawing buildings for their own enjoyment. Only on entering architecture school are they offered a framework conceived to organise, calibrate, expand and develop their interest in the subject.

Cook appreciated that getting the first year right would be fundamental to the success of his professorship. It would be the only shared experience of design teaching that undergraduate students would have before separating into different units, each with their own staff, agenda and interests. For several years before Cook's appointment, The Bartlett's first year was in the care of Christopher Woodward. A highly intelligent and austere Miesian, as well as an acute critic, he was not always sympathetic to the condition of 'wandering in a labyrinth of experiments', as UCL's first professor of architecture, Thomas Leverton Donaldson, presciently described the position of architecture in an academic context in 1841.[10] To borrow a concept from the philosopher Isaiah Berlin, Woodward was a hedgehog, 'relating everything to a single central vision... in terms of which [hedgehogs] understand, think and feel', while Pimenides is like a fox. In this analogy, foxes 'lead lives, perform acts and entertain ideas that are centrifugal rather than centripetal; their thoughts scattered or diffuse, moving on many levels, seizing upon the essence of a vast variety of experience and objects for what they are in themselves.'[11]

Many first-year programmes, indeed many entire architecture courses, have shown hedgehog-like characteristics: the École des Beaux-Arts owed much of its success to coercing students into precise prescriptions, while the critic and educator Reyner Banham noted the almost universal, always impervious way architecture schools' design studios acculturalised their students.[12] But Cook's tastes run to the eclectic, and with upwards of 100

---

10. Melvin and Sheil, *The Bartlett 175*, 2016, p. 7.
11. Isaiah Berlin, 'The Hedgehog and the Fox: An Essay on Tolstoy's View of History', *Russian Thinkers*, Penguin Classics, 2008, pp. 22–81. The essay's subtitle gives an indication of the subject matter, hence describing the concept as 'borrowed'.
12. See Reyner Banham, 'A Black Box: The Secret Profession of Architecture', written as his inaugural lecture as Sheldon H. Solow Professor in the History of Architecture at The Institute of Fine Arts at New York University but not delivered, published in Reyner Banham, *A Critic Writes: Selected Essays by Reyner Banham*, California University Press, 1997, pp. 292–9.

students in each year, from ever more diverse parts of the world, turning to a fox had a certain logic.

Pimenides brought an accumulation of diverse experiences to the role. Both sides of her family had a track record of academic achievement, her grandfathers as professors of science, and her parents as educationalists. But they were also steeped in Greek culture and mythology; her maternal grandfather, a professor of chemistry by day, but by calling, taste and intuition created an extraordinary home with buildings of classical, Byzantine and vernacular inspiration that evoked the mythology of the Olympian Gods. For Pimenides, there has never been an inherent incompatibility between science and myth. She believes that 'without science we are doomed, without myth we are depressed'.

London provides another series of places for Pimenides' teaching practice. In one sense it is a counterbalance to the mythology of place that comes from her experience in Greece. She first came to know the city as a student in the 1970s, and gradually discovered its richness through her own explorations, guided by people she encountered. She also began to intuit that London, sometimes in the most unlikely locations, had something of the mysteries of place that the great Greek classical sites have. Perhaps most apparent in her longstanding engagement with Sir John Soane's work, her appreciation of London is a vital element in her teaching programmes.

In both London and the Greek sites, Pimenides found different layers and levels of meaning. They might appear to be rocks on a mountainside or a derelict corner of a busy street, but knowing or investigating how they acquired their appearance opens up the possibility of metaphorical and allegorical, possibly even transcendental, significance as well as their literal state. These alternative readings allow students to make connections with their own experience and interests and so embed the sites, and the design projects set for them, in a broader frame of cultural reference.

The roles these locations play are distinct. The classical sites allude to an underlying cultural nexus of ideas, often nebulous and lacking definitive detail. In London, by contrast, it is often the minutiae that attract Pimenides' eye, the intricate solutions to everyday problems, the tiny and fragmentary objects that may nonetheless tell an important story. In this way, London becomes a tool for introducing individual architects and the specific challenges architecture faces. At some level, these architects and their works relate to the broader concerns of architectural history and so, in an elliptical vortex, to the classical sites and the architecture that was created on and in specific relationship to them.

For Pimenides none of this could make sense without a deliberately constructed and constantly nurtured concept of 'studio culture'. That concept is the culmination and amalgamation of the networks of people, places and objects that we discuss in the first three chapters. Studio culture is part physical – the spaces where design teaching operates and their furnishings and atmosphere – but also the social dynamic of the people who use these spaces: the students and staff. Underlying all this is a commitment to learning, based on loyalty, responsibility and above all trust. These may seem difficult terms in modern academia but they are essential to Pimenides' conception of architectural education. I liken these to what Harvard professor Henry Louis Gates Jr. described as 'pre-modern' virtues in an essay in *The New Yorker*,[13] and bear some relation to the 'governance syndrome', which the urban analyst Jane Jacobs defined in contrast to the 'commerce system' in her book *Systems of Survival: A Dialogue on the Moral Foundations of Commerce and Politics*.[14]

Reyner Banham's depiction of 'studio culture' in architecture schools as a 'black box' or 'tribal long room',[15] where initiates are inculcated with the mysteries of their tribe, could apply equally to Berlin's characterisation of hedgehogs or foxes, but with its prescriptive results tends more to the former. Pimenides' notion of studio culture is certainly about acculturing students into the world of architecture. The biblical reference in Níall McLaughlin's observation that Pimenides 'bears witness to what it is to be an architect' is deliberate. Rather than setting out a single course for a professional career, she aims to set out the challenges and offer tools that may help to overcome them. All this is worthless, however, without personal choice and commitment, and a possible admixture of another virtue that has gone out of fashion: faith.

Faith, for Pimenides, is the necessary precondition for risk. If students have no confidence that their endeavours will be treated seriously they are more likely to tend to a norm, especially if exemplars are set out. But if they have faith in the fairness and efficacy of the system they can experiment, assured that they will learn from failure, perhaps even more than success. As one of Pimenides' influences, the writer and educationalist Ken Robinson said, 'What we do know is, if you're not prepared to be wrong, you'll never come up with anything original.'[16]

---

13. Henry Louis Gates Jr., 'The End of Loyalty', *The New Yorker*, vol. 74, no. 3, 9 March 1998, p. 34.
14. Jane Jacobs, *Systems of Survival: A Dialogue on the Moral Foundations of Commerce and Politics*, Random House, 1992.
15. Banham, 'A Black Box', 1997.
16. Ken Robinson, 'Do Schools Kill Creativity?', *TED*, 2007, www.ted.com/talks/sir_ken_robinson_do_schools_kill_creativity.

Studio culture would be a series of empty gestures without people and the networks they bring and create to animate it. It also needs places to exist and nurture ideas, and objects to populate them. Pimenides has an extraordinary inquisitiveness about, and memory for, people. She likes to know where her students come from, how they chose The Bartlett, and how they form and dissolve groups and relationships. This would be trivial were it not an integral part of how she organises and steers them. She takes inspiration from conductor Gustavo Dudamel as an exemplar for directing diverse people with different skills to contribute to a collective endeavour.

One further theme merits its own chapter: Installations. Taking place at the end of the first term of the year, the installations are not the culmination of the programme, though they prefigure many of the desired outcomes. Installations have taken the form of a feast, with various courses served in a significant part of UCL's estate; a procession taking symbolic repossession of 22 Gordon Street, The Bartlett's historic home, after a two-year exile while it was refurbished; and a musical performance and kinetic installations on the canal in Hackney.

For many years there was a collaboration with Sir John Soane's Museum, which saw installations at Pitzhanger Manor and Lincoln's Inn Fields. These installations demonstrate the necessity of getting out of the studio. Typically, each project culminates in a series of installations, which can include performance, that temporarily transform an unprepossessing part of London, such as a forgotten corner of Spitalfields or an uninspiring slice of canal bank in Hackney, through installations. All these locations must be outside the studio. They carry within them ideas imbibed from studio culture and place them so they stand on their own. In this sense, each installation is a step for students on the journey to becoming an architect.

These themes – people, places, objects, installations and studio culture – are inter-related elements within Pimenides' teaching practice. This book discusses them in individual chapters, but as will become apparent, they are far from discrete entities and can only be properly understood in relation to each other. They are in a constant state of flux, but just as a conductor like Dudamel can create exquisite moments of temporary resolution, so Pimenides strives to guide students towards similar instances in their individual projects.

Images

0.1 A representative shelf, including personal items, work, and students' models, in Frosso Pimenides' year-one office at The Bartlett, 2013. Photo: Frosso Pimenides and Robert Newcombe.
0.2 The Piraeus Lion, Venice, November 2018. Photo: Frosso Pimenides.
0.3 Derelict Venetian façade, Heraklion, Crete, August 2019. Photo: Frosso Pimenides.
0.4 Hadrian's Villa, year-one field trip to Tivoli, January 2020. Photo: Frosso Pimenides.

Chapter 1:
People

FROSSO PIMENIDES: This chapter explores the many and varied ways in which people participate in my practice of teaching architecture. Both education and architecture – the two overarching subjects of this book – are essentially about people. Bring the two together under 'architectural education' and the importance of understanding the roles and relationships between people becomes really quite important.

Any architectural endeavour involves skills in dealing with people, and these are among the qualities that education should cultivate, strengthen and refine. Architecture is a complex profession; architects need to understand people in order to design for them. They must possess and cultivate the fundamental skills of being able to communicate and listen to others in parallel to collaborating with a wide range of other professions, in other words, working as part of a group.

To understand people is the first goal of architecture, which requires empathy. Buildings are there to make our lives better, but there is another vital element to thinking about people in the context of education and that is to help them discover their creative identities and processes. Our job is to support the development of students, to teach them to not be afraid of the implications of their abilities and perceptions, to discover what they can offer and imagine and how this can merge with previous experiences with teachers, family members, mentors and friends.

This attempt to understand how people interact in the context of architectural education has to start at the beginning: the moment a new cohort of students arrives at the start of the academic year. Each student is of course an individual and, unlike those beginning other courses of study, they have a wide range of educational and cultural experiences, with many arriving with more varied school leaving qualifications than students on most other university courses. Yet the critical task at this stage – and increasingly so if student numbers continue to rise and staff resources become more stretched – is to forge them into a group.

The group and its dynamic

FP: The year group has to have an internal dynamic that allows the free exchange of ideas without prejudice or reference to previous status, where all are treated as equals, which cannot happen without trust. Over nine months, this group of strangers – novice students – are invited into an academic family, where mutual trust makes a safe place for experiments, ideas, projects and events. It is this trust that gives students the confidence to undergo the necessarily huge learning curve, possibly the most intense of their careers. They are taught and learn a range of skills, and a lot is expected of them: first, to learn new drawing and making skills in order to express their ideas; second, to challenge and even completely reverse their methods of working to those learned in their secondary education;[1] third, to find out their strengths and weaknesses as people and to work on these; fourth, to encourage them to take the role of citizens as well as students; and fifth, to slowly understand the complexity of what an architect deals with – to be introduced to the group work that is an ongoing reality in a professional career and, ultimately, in designing a building. These explorations are only possible within a territory of mutual trust and loyalty between fellow students and tutors. The tutor-student relationship, having reached this level of loyalty and trust, is magical.

 The next piece in the jigsaw of how groups can work is empathy. Why is empathy so critical to an architect? If an architect has to deal with people and places, the primary obligation is to begin to understand them. To understand means to be patient enough to listen, think, digest, react, engage and communicate with another person. Empathy, in this sense, is entering someone's soul, mind and point of view, often completely different to your own. That presupposes an open mind and patience, and realising there is more than one approach to understanding the world we are in. To be able to see the world through someone else's eyes, and to think about it critically, is a great skill for an architect. Empathy can also cultivate imagination and broaden the fields of our immediate experience and horizon. Imagining other situations, possibilities and ways of seeing the world is the first and most critical quality to instil in a new architecture student's mind. Imaginative and constructive questioning is an important starting point. We endeavour to empower students to dare and be secure enough to run the risk of failure, and not be afraid to change things if needed.

---

1. See the educationalist Ken Robinson's criticism of school education for stifling creativity. Ken Robinson, 'Do Schools Kill Creativity?', *TED*, 2006, www.ted.com/talks/sir_ken_robinson_do_schools_kill_creativity.

JEREMY MELVIN: As Pimenides makes clear above, the understanding of people in general (humanity), and of certain individuals, forms a crucial part of her teaching practice. This may well be true of any serious educator, but it is worth probing further as her case has certain peculiarities. The people to whom she refers fall into three basic categories, with some overlaps between them: influences (relations, mentors and friends), colleagues, and students. Equally crucial to the individuals are the relationships between them, governed by emotions like trust, loyalty and empathy.

Together, her appreciation of people in general flows from her experience, going back to childhood, of dealing with individuals. It is from this that she identifies the need for empathy, trust and loyalty to form a disparate and diverse group of people – even if she has some choice over selecting colleagues, students, especially when they descend in cohorts of over 100, are necessarily random and diverse – into an effective dynamic.

By exploring how Pimenides uses the resulting set of experiences and principles to forge a working dynamic, we identify several different parts in this chapter. The first focuses on individuals; the second on the range of possible relationships between them, including their lives, personalities, experience and perception, as well as the strengths and weaknesses that they collectively have; while the third places Pimenides' largely intuitive thoughts on the operation of teams and leadership in the context of contemporary thinkers.

Family culture

JM: Among the most important formative influences on Pimenides' teaching practice are members of her own family, and the dynamic that existed between them. Several points are worth noting: first, she came from a family of educators. Her grandfathers were both professors in scientific subjects, her father founded a school in Athens and completed a PhD in education, and her mother also worked in education. This formed the seed of the academic family that is central to the role individual people play in Pimenides' teaching practice. It is both an analogue of a biological family and part of the connective tissue of studio culture. Both parents were closely involved with the British Council in Athens from its early days after World War II, and so Pimenides had encounters with a range of cultures from an early age.

By translating Virginia Woolf into Greek, Pimenides' mother revealed education as both an integral part of culture and an important means of access to its riches. The second point to be noted was made even more explicit by her maternal grandfather. As a professor of chemistry he brought a scientific understanding to the ground conditions of any given place, but to this he added a layer of cultural and mythological understanding by drawing on Ancient Greek lore. As we shall see, the power of landscape and the significance with which mythology imbues it, play a vital role in Pimenides' teaching practice.

FP: My grandfather, Nicolas Manthos, was an eccentric professor of chemistry. He was an idealist, a dreamer and a complete rebel, totally uncompromising. He was also an obsessive art collector, a painter, builder, heavy smoker, fighter, and a naughty, messy, and cheeky scientist. He treated a king in the same manner as a road sweeper. He was my favourite family member. I lost him when I was 15.

My grandfather introduced me to the world of Greek mythology, to such an extent that Hermes or Zeus were considered part of my childhood family. To him they were real presences in the Greek countryside, behind every ripple of wind and certainly every clap of thunder. My other debts to him are my knowledge of maths, chemistry, painting and history. Scribbling endlessly on old cigarette packets, filling his study bedroom with the smoke of his two-packs-a-day habit, he taught me to be curious and naughty, and took me for endless walks to the real countryside and his beloved ancient ruins. During the week, the same person could be a government advisor on Greek tobacco cultivation and quality controls, and then over the weekends would build castles and treehouses and shadow-puppet figures for his grandchild. Not an easy character, my grandma was a saint to sustain his fiery intolerance of stupidity and corruption. She protected him, built a shield of loving and supportive care, understood his genius qualities, and ignored his short temper. His peculiar and rarefied pursuits demonstrated many of the facets necessary in teaching architecture: the ability to dream and imagine; creating alternative realities by combining myth and science; and methods for keeping some of the more irritating conditions of being alive at bay.

While writing this book I have realised how much I owe to the heritage, upbringing, and ways of seeing the world that my parents embedded in my life, and how I share this with my students. The presence of our parents is felt in our mind, soul, daily habits, milestone situations and events, memories and imagination. Our formative years are deeply marked by a plethora of interwoven and conflicting emotions, stories, and vivid-yet-blurred fragmented memories of events that we carry in our souls for the rest of our lives. I was lucky enough to be surrounded by wonderful, devoted parents and grandparents. Their values and ways of thinking and dealing with people, to become instinctive and intuitive, were embedded in my mind; a solid driving force for giving me the patience, hope and determination to fight for what I believed in.

My father, George Pimenides, had the patience of a saint. He was cheeky and stubborn, naughty and rebellious, a real philosopher and a professional dreamer, and, for better or worse, a perfectionist with an obsession for antique cars, opera and old books. He loved repairing stuff in his beloved study, which was actually a garage retreat. He loved entertaining his fellow educator friends. He loved people and starting a conversation with strangers, he was also very proper and was good at disguising his hatred of small talk.

My father was perpetually nostalgic for his early teens in Istanbul, especially when remembering his feisty pet seagull Poupousis. He spent much of his free time in the darkroom, printing endless black-and-white photos, and would often run away from my mother to explore unknown territories in his beloved 1950s grey and white DKW rally car. He was incredibly curious about his own pursuits, yet was also a great listener to his teenage pupils. He found teaching a real joy in his role as headmaster of the American Community Schools (ACS) Middle School, and he adored and supported his cohort of 50 teachers. Like many other educationalists, he was repeatedly fighting bureaucracy and difficult parents, both at odds with what a teacher is trying to achieve. He was an enthusiastic idealist with rare skills of empathy, compassion, and collaboration.

After my father passed away, just as we were completing our first year-one installation at The Bartlett in 1990, a lot of articles poured in from all over the world. George Pimenides is best described with a quote from Kahlil Gibran's poem *The Farewell*, '... he gave much and knew not that he gave at all...'.[2] Passionate about education, he was an active listener and pushed students to seek answers within themselves. My father was also a great believer in Robert Frost's quote 'I am not a teacher, but an awakener'.[3] He was the eternal student, in search of better ways, like the clerk in Geoffrey Chaucer's *Canterbury Tales*, 'Gladly would he learn, and gladly teach'.[4] His colleague Donald Eichhorn said, 'George Pimenides was truly seeking to nurture the intellectual, spiritual, physical needs of youth, as they form their

---

2. Kahlil Gibran, 'The Farewell', 1923, *Academy of American Poets*, https://poets.org/poem/farewell-2, accessed 27 August 2021.
3. Generally attributed to the poet Robert Frost.
4 Geoffrey Chaucer, describing the 'clerk of Oxenford' in the prologue to *The Canterbury Tales*, line 308. First published, London, c.1400, with many subsequent editions including William Caxton 1476/1483 (first printed versions).

1.5

1.6

1.7

adult notions and values'.[5] His love of putting new ideas into practice, his continual questioning, and his abilities as a great and true leader, loved and respected by his faculty, were a wonderful example of something like the ideal educationalist to me. Single- and clear-minded, he nevertheless showed consideration for all opinions and enjoyed arguing endlessly with opposition, true to his hero Plato.

My mother, Maria, was a person of phenomenal intelligence and sensitivity; her time studying English literature at Oxford remained a memory throughout her life. She was a natural teacher, her teaching marked by amazingly theatrical performances. Sadly, she sacrificed her career to bring up her daughter and support her husband who was running a school with hundreds of pupils while in parallel working on his PhD. She had to take on the characteristics of a sergeant major in all operations of professional and family life, but she remained grounded in reality, irritatingly decisive, uncompromising to the bone, with endless energy and a very progressive outlook. She had little patience for opposition, until her departure from life at the age of 96 years. For her, Victorian principles of duty came before any pleasures in life, a fact that caused many family disagreements, and in my formative high school years pushed me to become something of an undercover rebel. She had the capacity to enthuse and motivate an entire town in minutes, yet her impatience caused some pain.

The alchemy of my parents formed the basis of a way of life, a daily philosophy of being-in-the-world that became the foundation for anything good that influenced me. I conspired secretly with my father, trying to make his voice heard at home, and to protect both of them from not compromising. They were two totally different individuals, often frustrating each other, but deeply devoted to one another. My parents could not have been more totally contradictory people, in their likes and dislikes, temperament, character, idea of fun, daily habits and routines, family origins and upbringing, the way they bonded with close friends, choice of food and wine or favourite ways to spend a melancholic Sunday afternoon in the centre of Athens. Their families originated from across the Greek diaspora, including Constantinople (Istanbul), Pontus, Crete, Lavrion and Epirus, before finally converging on Athens. Both had a love of English literature, which drove their enthusiasm in their student days during World War II, George in Edinburgh and Maria in Oxford. They met during a trip organised by the British Council in Athens to

5. Donald H. Eichhorn, *Middle Ground*, vol. XX, no. 1, International and American Middle School Association, Athens, 1991, p. 5.

the tiny Greek island of Poros, straight after the war. What kept them going was a fighting spirit for their ideals, a huge sense of duty, and love for their jobs – both had a ruthless determination to focus on a target and accomplish their goal. They went through a lot of rough rides in life, but their fighting spirit always united them in stressful times. For me, they were the exemplary 'prisoners of hope'.[6] Their sense of civic and family duty, and their belief that teaching and real learning presupposes a level of deep trust, loyalty, and empathy, is the best gift they could ever have shared with me.

The academic family

JM: Given this background, when Pimenides came to London to study, creating a new family from academic connections was a logical move. The first members of this family were teachers at the Polytechnic of Central London (PCL),[7] the head of department, Allen Cunningham, and a wonderfully generous young New Zealander and his wife, John and Avril Hunt. Cunningham had worked for Le Corbusier and Marcel Breuer and made clear his affinity for mainstream modernism. He exuded a sense of style, dress and behaviour presented in the films Le Corbusier made about his buildings.[8] In them, life, art and work are all connected, including calibrating choice of colour and clothes. Not surprisingly, given the strength of her family ties and the charismatic generosity of the group of people she encountered when she relocated to London, Pimenides' instinct was to fashion an 'academic family' as an analogue to her blood family. This was one of the seeds for her future career.

FP: John Hunt taught me the importance and magic of place and territory, and initiated me into a super analytical and rational, yet very inspiring, way of design thinking and practice. At weekends John and Avril Hunt introduced me to their favourite hobbies, visiting National Trust houses, as well as making hippy-folk outfits. Our bonding lasted well beyond my first year in learning what it is to be an architecture student. The teacher that had the most profound influence upon me, however, was my second-year tutor, the Oregon hippy, cowboy and dreamer Don Genasci, who was tough, yet very emotional, and passionate about architecture. He and his wife Sharon regularly invited me to share a home-cooked Sunday lunch at their Primrose

---

6. Widely cited by Archbishop Desmond Tutu, originating in the Bible: Zechariah, chapter 9 verse 12.
7. Colloquially known as the Poly, now the University of Westminster.
8. Beatriz Colomina, *Privacy and Publicity: Modern Architecture as Mass Media*, The MIT Press, 1996. See chapters 'Photography', pp. 77–140, and 'Window', pp. 283–336.

Hill flat, full of books and eclectic collected items. Genasci taught me that architecture is first about ideas and instinct, beyond meticulous drawings and models, and is all about life and people. He taught us what team spirit means by training us, his students, to volunteer, run soup kitchens, and rebel if things did not work out. He initiated me in the loves of his life that sprang from his appreciation of the beauty of geometry: the amazing 17th-century Italian architect Francesco Borromini, 20th-century Finnish architect Alvar Aalto and the rigorous structure of early music, to which he added the Architectural Association (AA), leather boots, rare old second-hand books, good food, dreaming and the sense of fulfilment when designing and constructing a beautiful plan.

After graduating from my diploma I could not wait to start practising architecture. Upon returning to Athens I was immersed in all sorts of urban design and building projects. I really experienced the magic of being an architect when I designed and built my first building, just outside the city. It took three years to design and eight months to build, and is described in more detail in chapter three. Then, suddenly, I received an invitation from PCL to run an undergraduate unit, and that was how I was self-initiated and dropped in the middle of the ocean of teaching. This was followed by various positions in the undergraduate and postgraduate departments at the University of Cambridge, University of Leicester, Kingston University, and the AA.

JM: In the preceding section Pimenides describes how, when she came to London, she created a new set of ties with a group that was more or less strangers to her, but which replicated or adapted the conventions of family life, such as weekend outings and Sunday lunches. In this way, her extraordinary family in Greece became the model for her expanding intellectual and social horizons as a student. Given this, it is not entirely surprising that she was able to return to London some years after graduating and returning to Greece.

Initially, PCL was the centre. Students tended to live close to it and Pimenides had a room at the top of Luxborough Tower, which rises from the same podium as the academic buildings. Other polytechnic buildings grew the network along and south of Marylebone Road, but a decisive expansion came with a project for a community playground in Islington, more or less in a straight line along Euston Road and then Pentonville Road.

In the late 1980s, Pimenides worked at architects and designers Conran Roche, who were then based in nearby Fitzroy Square, more or less midway between The Bartlett and PCL, and at the AA, a similar distance to the south of that axis. Many years later her son Uilleac would study classical music at the Royal Academy of Music on Marylebone Road, adding another layer of engagement with this district of London. In this way, her sense of place expanded from the territory of PCL outwards to the rest of London, especially through the animation of her relationships with the people she encountered.

The professional family

JM: At the AA, Pimenides was a unit master in Intermediate Unit 1, when the charismatic chair Alvin Boyarsky tried to dissuade her from accepting Peter Cook's invitation to teach at The Bartlett, shortly after Cook was appointed professor there in 1990.[9] Not far beyond that circle was another one around the sensitive and subtle thought emanating from Joseph Rykwert and Dalibor Vesely,[10] strongly influenced by phenomenology. It was initially based at the University of Essex, then the AA and subsequently at the University of Cambridge. Pimenides first encountered Rykwert and Vesely during the MPhil programme they were running, which she took after graduating from her Architecture Part I course. In those years, the course was taught in the basement kitchen of the Sir John Soane's Museum. As she remembers: 'Those intense sessions and debates in that 18th-century kitchen, I found fascinating, if profoundly perplexing. It was great fun wandering amongst the ghosts of that era, squeezed in between cooking pots and manuscripts!' Such is the serendipity behind the origins of the network of people that Pimenides has forged to fulfil her teaching practice at The Bartlett.

As outlined above, the individuals who influenced Pimenides began with her immediate family, as with most people. Yet this grew and mutated when she came to London to study architecture, where she started to consider her teachers, colleagues and collaborators as part of some kind of family as well, during her student days and in the first years of her academic career in London. Another twist came when she was appointed to run The Bartlett's first year in 1990. In this managerial position, her network had to

9. Alvin Boyarsky was chair of the Architectural Association from 1971 until his death in 1990. One of the most significant architectural educationalists of his time, he employed Pimenides to teach there for several years before she moved – against his advice and wishes – to The Bartlett, where he had himself taught in the 1960s.
10. Joseph Rykwert is an influential figure in contemporary architectural thought. Rykwert left Warsaw for the UK in 1939 where he was educated at Charterhouse. He studied architecture during World War II at The Bartlett and the Architectural Association. He taught at the Royal College of Art in London and in Ulm, and was founding professor of art history at the University of Essex before moving to the University of Pennsylvania. Rykwert was awarded the 2014 RIBA Royal Gold Medal for Architecture. Dalibor Veseley left Prague in 1968. He became a colleague of Joseph Rykwert at the University of Essex, before moving to Cambridge University, where he became a much-loved teacher, providing intellectual substance to the architecture department.

1.8

1.9

1.10

1.11

1.12

1.13

take in the teaching colleagues for whom she was responsible for managing and appointing. During her first years in London, Pimenides' expanded academic family began to nurture her evolution into a teacher and her appointment at The Bartlett brought this to fruition. These networks and relationships, their corollaries and offshoots, formed the basis from which she developed her approach to first-year teaching alongside her co-directors Graeme Sutherland, Patrick Weber, Nat Chard, Max Dewdney and other colleagues.

Over time her network grew to include various role models who, while not part of a network as such, as there is no mutual exchange of ideas or acquaintanceship, have nonetheless promulgated ideas that shape Pimenides' thinking. Here we try to reveal the varying nature of networks and how people have helped to shape her teaching practice and notion of studio culture, and how she interacts with the places she invokes. As we have seen, the structure of Pimenides' family network infused intellectual interests and the concept of education into otherwise normal family relationships. Her systems of social relations more or less invert this, with intellectual ideas animating them while retaining the character of familial structures.

When Pimenides arrived at The Bartlett in 1990 she says that she vaguely knew three people: Philip Tabor, David Dunster and the man she describes as 'the legendary phenomenon called Peter Cook', himself recently appointed as professor and who had in turn appointed her. She remembers that the refreshing sense of freedom found in the university environment encompassed her, which she welcomed after being completely immersed for many years at the AA – a private academy that only teaches architecture.

When Cook offered her the job, the message was crystal clear: she had total freedom to do anything she thought a year-one course needed, as long as she 'delivered the goods', as she recalls. The trust and encouragement to dare and take risks motivated and enthused her. She never got bored. She loved Cook's dedication, energy and gutsy approach to life, and they supported each other through their 'common love for weird and unexpected, but not comfortable things'. In the mission to enthuse young people to dare and achieve unforeseen territories, the ship had a captain who was a dedicated leader, not a manager seeking safety.

Each of these experiences contributed to the formation of Pimenides' Bartlett teaching programme, but Peter Cook's mandate was the first step. The second came in several ways from the almost diametrically opposite character of David Dunster, already a powerful figure at The Bartlett, who had a hand in Cook's appointment as professor.

FP: In the early 1990s there were two totally different, though both charming, men on the first floor of Wates House, as The Bartlett's home at 22 Gordon Street was then known. Peter Cook and David Dunster were both devoted, fanatic advocates of architecture, who hated political correctness and had the immense courage to say what they thought. They were both totally and electrifyingly inspirational. Their heated discussions in crits and debates were so inspirational for the students: they showed passion, a heroic commitment to one's beliefs, and that respect for opposing views is vital and fundamental.

I met David long before Peter as he gave me my first part-time teaching job at Kingston. Many years later, when I had just been offered the job at The Bartlett, I developed the programme for my first year of teaching while I was renting his flat – he was on sabbatical in the States during the summer of 1990. David's loyalty and devotion to his friends was rare. He remains vivid in my mind for his immaculate sense of style, uncompromising devotion to his students, a sharp but kind sarcasm, enjoying people's company, endless debates, not being patronising, and his generosity of mind, soul and spirit. His motto 'if you have no idea, draw someone else's thought and see what comes of it' inspired me as I hunkered down to work in his Victorian kitchen, asking myself: how does one introduce people to architecture? His kitchen was a quiet place with lovely cooking pots, a huge Victorian table and a white ceramic sink.

Once I started teaching at The Bartlett, various other personalities joined my network. The dean was the late Pat O'Sullivan, who generously welcomed me into the department and was constantly trying to convince me that the controversial 'joint project' between architects, planners and construction managers was a good idea. In those early days, realising the 'joint project' was part of our annual installation, described in chapter five. During those years, Philip Tabor ran the architecture school with Peter Cook, creating an amazing alchemy of personalities and complementary skills. After debates early on about the cost of year one, Tabor became the most positive and profound mentor that anyone would have wished for, a trusted and loyal colleague whose support and care over the years was invaluable. The first person I spoke to as I took my new job, however, was an introverted, charming man called Adrian Forty, a wonderful architectural historian whose wide-ranging knowledge and insight into the nature of architecture contributed to the teaching programme as it evolved. We used to share ideas while brewing tea in the tiny kitchen on the first floor.

Since Peter Cook and Philip Tabor's era, deans of the faculty Pat O'Sullivan, Christine Hawley, Alan Penn, and Christoph Lindner have been immensely supportive and encouraging, and the directors of the school, Iain Borden, Marcos Cruz, and at present Bob Sheil, have supported and motivated with their various contributions to year-one education. It is humbling to think about how all of these very different characters have supported the teaching team over the years.

Over the 30 years of running the first year, my concept of an academic family has developed into a tool for students' learning, as well as managing staff. In October 1990 I arrived at UCL and presented the philosophical intentions and programme for the year to an unknown audience, my first ever year-one group. There was no confidence on either side, no sense of belonging and knowing each other, and it felt really intimidating – I was probably visibly nervous. Over the first three months, the students and staff managed to break the barrier of distance and shyness, gradually making fools of ourselves in the process of making and experimenting, and discovering what architecture is and what university education should be. By December we had managed to occupy eight locations within UCL for one day to install and perform our first ever year-one installation project, which was known as 'The Feast'. When I lost my father a few weeks later, that specific group of people, my students, provided me with the love and support I needed to carry on functioning in those difficult moments. A bond amongst some of the group is still strong today, more than 30 years later.

Given the formative and fragile nature of the first year in architectural education, the personalities and skills of the people it is entrusted to are critical. Between them they must have a mix of qualities appropriate to taking on the challenge of initiating students to architecture. How do we find these special personalities? To nurture the development and flourishing of a first-year student, teaching them to ask questions and not provide answers, pointing out how an architect might look at things differently, and cultivating their imagination and design visions, provides the tutor with a huge sense of fulfilment.

Structure

FP: Another vital point is the year-one structure. It is totally different to the unit system that prevails in later years, in that the entire group is taught together for part of the programme and in small groups that can change throughout. The range of approaches that tutors provide is critical. We need a variety of skills and personalities that can work together to teach a whole year group and small groups, and at times offer one-to-one tuition responding to students' queries and uncertainties. This is a continuous double-act: being firm as well as helping to develop students' skills, minds and souls. Continuity and stability are important but on occasion new teaching personalities can be mutually challenging and supportive, contributing to possible alchemies. The exposure to a range of teachers reinforces the gradual build-up of confidence and allows them to learn a range of skills, but above all it teaches them that there is always more than one answer to a question or approach to a problem. This makes a powerful antidote to the monoculture that encroaches and risks suffocating a lot of architecture institutions nowadays.

I am grateful to the school for trusting me to select a diverse range of colleagues for first-year design teaching. We do not only choose these people for their qualifications and performance at interview, we choose them because they have proven themselves as designers and have a passion for sharing architectural explorations with students. They love to help, to challenge their own views, to listen to mad ideas, and to share their skills. Over the years this has been a gradual exercise in bonding, dedication, loyalty, and solidarity to our common cause. We have learnt to adapt and accept personal differences and frictions, even using them positively. What has bonded us is that we all have the same values regarding quality of teaching, standard of good design, and pleasure in discovery when working with students at the beginning of their architectural education.

Over these three decades it is possible to identify several distinctive eras, which were largely defined by dominant personalities and colleagues in the teaching team. Further to this, the workshop team became known as The Bartlett Manufacturing and Design Exchange (B-made) in 2012, during the transition of leadership from Abi Abdolwahabi to Peter Scully. B-made supports a wide sphere of academic and technical staff.

The initial years (1990–2000), working with my co-director Graeme Sutherland – a patient, deep thinker and exceptionally clear designer – were hugely exciting and focused on experimenting with what year-one education is. The vibrant team working alongside us were generous, charming and dedicated philosophers, optimists and eccentrics. With only 45 students initially, subsequently growing to 60 or more, it was easier to maintain course quality and balance our work, than it has been with groups of over 100 in recent years.

During the second era (2000–14) we slowly built up a wonderful studio culture (see chapter four), with my then co-director Patrick Weber. An inspirational designer and maker, dedicated to the bone to education, Weber is able to turn his hand to almost anything. Thanks to his commitment, we developed a highly compact, structured and sophisticated year-one course. Like all worthwhile things in life, it is hard to maintain the endless stamina to deal with the challenges of academia, a constant high standard of student work, and a commitment from staff to develop students' interests. In that era, wonderful new colleagues entered our world, many of whom still teach with us today.

The third era was when Nat Chard joined as co-director in 2014, at a transitional time when we packed up our lives at Wates House and emigrated to our temporary studios at 140 Hampstead Road. The arrival of Chard, a phenomenally inquisitive mind and extraordinarily inventive designer, together with the move, allowed us to experiment and expand in different areas of design and teaching. During my sabbatical absence, the wonderfully enthusiastic and eccentric designer Carlos Jiménez joined Nat in his endeavours, as well as a great raft of new tutors.

Since 2017, my co-director has been our former student Max Dewdney, now a successful designer, architect and devoted educator. Dewdney has joined me in a job that is getting increasingly difficult, due to our rapidly expanding student cohort. Dewdney belongs to a rare breed of people with both talent and integrity. He is a veteran of fighting unnecessary bureaucracy and is, like me, a prisoner of hope. Together – and with our team of associates Gavin Robotham, Lucy Leonard, Emmanouil Stavrakakis, Stefan Lengen, and our tutors – we are constantly reflecting upon the strengths and weaknesses of what we have established so far in year one.

In recent years, radical cultural and educational shifts in secondary and higher education are increasingly threatening students' latent creativity and imagination, in an era when acquiring sophisticated skills is highly valued. Another of our biggest changes and challenges over the years has been adapting to a growth in student numbers, from 60 to over 120. Growing size in any organisation is a tricky business. Growth can occur for all sorts of reasons, including diversity, critical mass and financial stability. Once an organisation or institution, particularly in education, starts to grow, immense energy has to be devoted to maintaining its quality, ethos, principles, ambitions and overall vision. Connectivity and communication are key foundations for this expanding world. Common ground and diversity need to exist in parallel, but that requires vertical as well as horizontal management.

This is a major challenge in most growing institutions. We, the academics, managers, students and support staff, risk being overcome by bureaucratic overload, when in fact we are often generating the additional workload ourselves. Sharing and teamwork is the pathway to a free-flowing and efficient culture.

Alchemy

FP: It is very rare for a student, particularly in their initial year of being alone in a city and starting an academic course in an unknown subject, to ask for help unless they trust and value their tutor. This relationship takes time to build up, and it is all based upon a gradual and mutual exchange, dialogue, and spirit of generosity and care. It is a constant game of ping pong, a dialectic relationship, where both student and tutor participate equally, where one member throws in an idea and the other takes it further, questioning and transforming it into something unknown and better. We cannot expect students to take risks, experiment and be inventive when failures occur if we are not able to learn from them and treat them as opportunities for success ourselves. Once they take the first baptism into these deep waters then they can start to fly. When we treat students as partners and collaborators we can research and explore ideas in parallel. When that happens, on the one hand it allows them to feel confident and strong enough to experiment on their own, but on the other we can offer help whenever they need it. At that point, real learning – the exchange of ideas and skills – can take place, enabling them to develop on their own. This chapter attempts to explain how people can be selected and organised to generate this sort of dynamic or alchemy. A great deal of what we have become and what we have achieved, our deep sources of inspiration and motivation, come from the people that have been part of our lives.

The leader and the network

JM: The purpose of this section is to indicate how Pimenides' ideas about team dynamics and leadership may fit into a contemporary context. It is important to note that her ideas are often intuitive and derived from experience rather than theoretical analysis, though she absorbs ideas from many sources. She is, in essence, struggling with one of the central issues in contemporary education: how to empower individual students to identify and understand their own potential, and then to achieve it for themselves. She sees both education and architecture as part of a cultural continuum, not as isolated phenomena. For this reason, the empowerment she seeks to engender in her students is profoundly related to the culture around them – some of that culture, as sentient beings in the 21st century, they share – but each has an individual set of experiences and background, as well as varying ability and interests, that temper, refine and hone it.

Pimenides makes many references to the educationalist Sir Ken Robinson, and in particular his belief that most contemporary education systems militate against creativity. This underpins her statement that one of the most important things for a first-year student is to throw off some of what they have learnt at school. We shall probe this further, before turning to a commentator on management, whom she also cites, Simon Sinek. Finally, we shall propose some points that place Pimenides' teaching practice as part of a cultural continuum with reference to the historian Niall Ferguson. Though she does not refer to Ferguson, his thoughts on hierarchies and networks echo hers, showing that they are not an isolated phenomenon.

Robinson made his views explicit about the importance of creativity in, and its exclusion from, conventional education in a TED talk in 2006.[11] He articulates many of Pimenides' points about the importance of creativity, and by lamenting its exclusion from school education he highlights the challenge she faces in reintroducing it to first-year students. One of Robinson's central points is that all children are potentially creative. 'All kids have talent but we squander it' he remarks, and we are 'educating people out of their creative capacities [at school].' He goes on to celebrate the importance of creativity to society as it engenders 'critical interaction of different inter-disciplinary ways of seeing things'.[12] So Pimenides' thoughts on creativity have support from one of its most significant advocates, giving her approach to teaching the first year of an architectural course significance outside the world of architecture and its education. Pimenides' views on leadership are defined but subtle. She says:

If spirits are low, I need to boost them… if there is panic or low morale, or exhaustion, I need to act as a crutch to support, enthuse and inspire the various tutors and students, telling them that they should never give up. Intuition and rational thinking are necessary forces, running in parallel at all times.

11 & 12. Robinson, *Do Schools Kill Creativity?*, 2006.

Pimenides expands her concept of the role along the lines of Níall McLaughlin's comment that she 'bears witness to what it is to be an architect':

I need to provide the glue, the cohesion that is needed to keep the year-one boat afloat. I am always looking for tutors very different to each other, so the students understand that it is the combination of all of us, however eccentric, that brings the magic into our year-one family. None of the tutors individually is perfect, but collectively we should cover most critical qualities needed in year-one teaching. One might be a brilliant designer, one a brilliant teacher, one might be a maker, one might be a thinker, one might be a pessimist, or one might believe in magic. It is my job to bring the best out of each of them, and most of all, to make them feel at ease with each other. We have the most challenging yet the most fun mission in architectural education: to introduce people to architecture. We are a team and a family with all its virtues and vices. We need to learn to help and support each other's students, in bringing out their individualities as well as teaching them the basic skills.

A leader, Pimenides explains, needs to inspire rather than dictate, and to act as catalyst in an alchemy of various situations, personalities, strengths and weaknesses. As Sinek explains in his book *Start With Why: How Great Leaders Inspire Everyone to Take Action* (2009), the reason behind any act is to motivate and inspire people. Subsequently, *what* we need to do and *how* we achieve that will naturally follow. A leader should never hold back their team, but trust them and encourage them into making achievements in unknown territories:

In this approach it is important that the entire team owns and cares about this why, they feel responsible in contributing to the overarching goal, which gives them a sense of achievement, and not a short-term incentive. They are led by someone but they do not act as slaves following commands, they take the role of partners.[13]

Pimenides says:

Teamwork is a key component of an architect's life, and it has to be slowly nurtured right from the moment we embark that world, in the formative first year. A leader without the right team does not exist! Trusting team members' opinions is vital in a healthy collaboration and coexistence. Learning to listen,

---

13. Simon Sinek, *Start With Why: How Great Leaders Inspire Everyone to Take Action*, Portfolio, 2009.

question, disagree, argue, delegate, accept other points of view and not micro-manage is the foundation of a healthy partnership. This is not easy, but worth fighting for. Empathy, loyalty, trust and risk-taking are all part of healthy, productive and successful collaborations, amongst the hugely diverse backgrounds of people and skills they can offer.

To facilitate this, students should trust that their tutors are willing to offer protection when necessary. In Sinek's second book, *Leaders Eat Last: Why Some Teams Pull Together and Others Don't* (2017), he summarises this view of leadership:

Leaders are the ones who run headfirst into the unknown. They rush toward danger. They put their own interests aside to protect us or to pull us into the future. Leaders would sooner sacrifice what is theirs to save what is ours. And they would never sacrifice what is ours to save what is theirs.[14]

This echoes the view of the American World War II airborne forces general James Garvin, who claimed that officers should be the first to jump out of aeroplanes and the last in the food line. In our context, leaders – normally tutors – rush into the unknown to open up territory for students to follow. To appreciate this, we will have to explore the concept of networks a bit further, before Pimenides outlines how the collaboration needed to produce the annual end-of-year show captures, in condensed form, how the dynamics between people can lead to a successful outcome.

Niall Ferguson has considered networks in his book *The Square and the Tower: Networks, Hierarchies and the Struggle for Global Power* (2017).[15] He outlines how network theory originated in 18th-century mathematics, but only started to be used to study social relationships in the early 20th century.[16] Shoehorning various complicated issues to make them fit his duality of networks (squares) and hierarchies (towers), he uses his hypothesis to explain various contemporary conundrums. In this outline, leadership, loyalty and trust – identified above as key phenomena in educational relationships – all come to the fore.

Networks form, or at least assume, significance when they become systems for exchanging something that one part has which is useful to others. That is as true of trading networks as of those in education. For Ferguson,

14. Simon Sinek, *Leaders Eat Last: Why Some Teams Pull Together and Others Don't*, Portfolio, 2017.
15. Niall Ferguson, *The Square and the Tower: Networks and Power, from the Freemasons to Facebook*, Penguin, 2018.
16. Ferguson, *The Square and the Tower*, 2018, pp. 24–9.

'homophily', which he defines as 'our tendency to gravitate to people similar to us', might 'be regarded as the first law of social networks',[17] but this is problematic in education. If all the members of a network are similar it is hardly likely to encourage innovative thinking or interaction with students who do not fit the norm. Hierarchy, one possible form of leadership, is the other side of Ferguson's duality. He sees an 11th-century mural of *The Last Judgment* in the cathedral of Santa Maria Assunta on the Venetian island of Torcello as the archetypal depiction of hierarchy. Noting the etymology of 'hierarchy' – literally 'rule of a high priest' – he points out the mural's five tiers, from Christ at the top to hell at the bottom.[18]

For Pimenides, leadership is less prescribed and goes as far as avoiding hierarchy. She is much closer to Sinek, whose view of leadership is encapsulated in his title *Leaders Eat Last*. But leadership is still vital for group work to succeed.

She argues that a successful group combines leadership with trust and loyalty. The Harvard professor Henry Louis Gates Jr. sets out a fascinating thesis for the relationship between leadership, trust and loyalty in his essay 'The End of Loyalty' (1998). Loyalty, he argues, belongs to a group of 'pre-modern' virtues that includes faith and trust, which the utilitarian side of modernism treats with contempt, especially when they encourage people to save their grandmother from a burning house when they might have saved the Archbishop of Canterbury from a fiery fate.[19] A utilitarian calculus would suggest that the Archbishop's survival would bring happiness to a greater number than the grandmother. Acknowledging the absurdity of such a conclusion, Gates suggests that there may be more life in the old, semi-feudal virtues, which allow for human emotion, than most of the rationalism-fetishising modern world recognised.

A few years earlier, urban analyst and commentator Jane Jacobs, in her book *Systems of Survival: A Dialogue on the Moral Foundations of Commerce and Politics* (1992), identified similar 'pre-modern' virtues to Gates, grouping them together in the 'guardian syndrome', which she contrasts with a 'commerce syndrome'.[20] The first includes virtues such as tradition, ostentation and respect for hierarchy, while the latter includes thrift, industriousness and efficiency. Where Gates argued that the 'guardian syndrome-like virtues' were out of kilter with the modern world, Jacobs

17. Ferguson, *The Square and the Tower*, 2018, p. 26.
18. Ferguson, *The Square and the Tower*, 2018, p. 21 and plate 1.
19. Henry Louis Gates Jr., 'The End of Loyalty', *The New Yorker*, 9 March 1998.
20. Jane Jacobs, *Systems of Survival: A Dialogue on the Moral Foundations of Commerce and Politics*, Vintage, 1994.

argued that both syndromes were alive and relevant, but accounted for different behavioural patterns as individuals tend to subscribe to one or other set of moral precepts.[21] Pimenides' teaching practice has affinities with both of Jacobs' syndromes. Loyalty, honour and fortitude are virtues she values, while she would shun some of the others, such as exclusivity and vengeance. From the commerce syndrome, openness to invention, initiative and enterprise, collaboration and optimism all chime. Easy collaboration with strangers is another welcome characteristic, but for her this can only happen within a positive studio culture that welcomes and acculturises those from outside its circle.

What this very cursory discussion shows is that Pimenides' ideas about education, leadership, trust and loyalty, and their importance in teamwork, do not exist in a vacuum. These ideas are at the centre of important debates in education, management, and in understanding how societies operate. Her first-year programme is a vital stepping-stone for architectural students and a cornerstone of The Bartlett's success over the last few decades,[22] and it is also a small but integral part of the school's culture.

FP: At the end of the academic year, the annual Summer Show (end-of-year exhibition) is the first time that the first-year students experience what it entails to share in public their various achievements. For the first-year cohort this is a time of collaboration, learning new skills, and celebration, rather than a pure act of exhibiting their individual work. It is a period of learning new techniques and experimenting with unknown methods of fabrication, sharing knowledge and learning from each other's diverse strengths and talents. This coming together after the intensity of their exam period, the team dynamics, and the ups and downs of collaboration, provide opportunities to hone some of the skills needed in their future lives as professionals, as well as members of society. It is a period of finding out more about each other, and a rewarding time to share their successful outcomes.

21. Jacobs evokes Thorstein Veblen's seminal sociological text *The Theory of the Leisure Class*, 1899. Veblen noted ostentation, respect for hierarchy and tradition to be among the behavioural traits of the 'leisure class', i.e. aristocracy.
22. The 2021 QS World University Rankings by subject rates The Bartlett second in the world for Architecture and the Built Environment. The same survey ranks UCL eighth equal among higher education institutions in the world.

Chapter 1 images
Photographs courtesy of Frosso Pimenides unless otherwise stated.

1.1 The Amphitheatre at Epidavros, July 2017.
1.2 Maria and George Pimenides with young Frosso.
1.3 Pimenides' family in the Garden at Ekali, Athens.
1.4 George Pimenides alongside Frosso Pimenides' grandmother Danae Manthos. A typical late evening family moment in the living room, which was a constant study space, Athens, c.1980s.
1.5 UCL graduation photo, c.1990s. Clockwise from top left: Professor Peter Cook, student Stephen Tierney, Professors Philip Tabor, Pat O'Sullivan, Christine Hawley and Frosso Pimenides.
1.6 Bartlett alumnae Ruth Allan and Aoife Considine with Uilleac Pimenides Whelan, London, 2002.
1.7 Peter Cook and Frosso Pimenides, 13 December 2016, upon arrival at 22 Gordon Street. Later, the first crit of the six installations forming that year's year-one group project took place, inaugurating the newly refurbished building.
1.8 Professor Adrian Forty, London, February 2015.
1.9 Professor Nat Chard, then co-director of year one, at Greenwich Beach, 2015.
1.10 The Bartlett's 'rock and anchor', security guard Donatus Onyido, with the year-one installation in the stairwell at 22 Gordon Street, at the end of the evening, 13 December 2016.
1.11 Bartlett colleague Roberto Ledda, whom Pimenides describes as the 'loyal and trusted veteran and guard of our studios and models, in the various buildings we have occupied', here, transporting a year-one model, one of the first of the year-one installation projects to utilise digital manufacturing, 134 Hampstead Road, October 2014.
1.12 Pimenides' former teacher, mentor, friend, Bartlett alumnus and RIBA Gold Medallist, Professor Joseph Rykwert, in his study, 4 August 2019.
1.13 Pimenides with students at the ceremonial burning of the models, part of the year-one installation trilogy 'Encore–Playback' (see chapter five), 9pm, 12 December 2016.

Chapter 2:
Places

JEREMY MELVIN: The concept of 'place' is persistent and important in contemporary architecture, and comes in many senses and forms. Joseph Rykwert has written about the 'seduction of place' in his eponymous book *Remembering Places: A Memoir* (2017).[1] Seductive places might also be related to Richard Sennett's argument that the public realm of a city can nurture our wellbeing, expressed in his book *The Conscience of the Eye: The Design and Social Life of Cities* (1992).[2] Aldo van Eyck, an integral member of Team X, a group of architects who challenged the central tenets of modernist convention after World War II, encapsulated this challenge in claiming that 'place' was more important than 'space'.[3] In this, he meant that the specifics of a particular location trumped the abstract generics of 'space' as a universal concept, a conclusion he reached through significant anthropological research. Such influences have trickled into present day practice and policy, where 'place-making' has become a sub-branch of architecture. The influential architect and urbanist Sir Terry Farrell claims 'place is the client'.[4]

Frosso Pimenides believes that a particular layered understanding of place and places is essential to architectural design. Teaching students how to analyse and appreciate places is, therefore, an essential part of architectural education. This chapter explores Pimenides' appreciation of places – some well known, others not – and how this oscillates between fiction, imagination and reality. The chapter starts by setting out why place is so important in architectural education and goes on to discuss places she has used in her 30 years at The Bartlett: sites in London and other cities visited as part of the field-trip programme, and concluding with descriptions of places

1. Joseph Rykwert, *Remembering Places: A Memoir*, Routledge, 2017.
2. Richard Sennett, *The Conscience of the Eye: The Design and Social Life of Cities*, Faber & Faber, 1990.
3. Aldo van Eyck, 'Whatever space and time mean, place and occasion mean more', cited in Hans Ibelings, 'Aldo van Eyck (1918–1999)', *The Architectural Review*, 17 December 2012, www.architectural-review.com/essays/reputations/aldo-van-eyck-1918-1999.
4. This is stated often by Terry Farrell in articles and lectures.

that have inspired and influenced her teaching practice. In Pimenides' teaching, a range of media is employed to investigate the qualities of places: photography, film, sound recordings, written notes, technical as well as expressive drawings, rubbings, spontaneous and final drawings. Above all, the process of recording is not a tick-box but rather a tool to cultivate a student's critical abilities in understanding a place.

Pimenides' concept of place is heavily influenced by classical mythology, and in particular the association between physical characteristics and derived metaphysical attributes and explanations. She puts a particular twist on the familiar architectural concept of place or the familiar phrase 'sense of place'. For her, places actively embody certain cultural ideas, which are not necessarily obvious but are latent and awaiting discovery. Places have a visceral, physical reality but also traces of memory, illusion and allusion, which are different for every person who comes into contact with them, and which provide the basis for stimulating creative thought in the minds of individual students. This chapter explores the origins of her concept of place, how it has evolved and the role it performs in her teaching practice, and offers a brief analysis of the intellectual context into which her ideas fit.

Places and their invisible ghosts

FROSSO PIMENIDES: In introducing students to architectural education, several questions come to mind: Why are people and places so important? How and what do we teach about place? Architecture is taught in a variety of spaces, not only in a classroom or studio space. An architect's first job is to look, so they understand the place they are asked to 'intervene in' by building something. This act of intervention needs brains, patience, instinct, and knowledge of various topics and disciplines. Tutors need to think critically. Sometimes we need to dare and take risks, other times we need to do very little. Sometimes we need to destroy a place and be courageously radical, at others we need to listen and do nothing.

Architecture is taught not only on the drawing board in workshops and classrooms, but in various locations in the city, the countryside and in the open. Sometimes it is taught in the back of a truck, on a donkey, in a workshop, on a rooftop, in a church, on top of a mountain, in the street, on a bus, in an architect's office, on a muddy building site, up a tree, or in a café. Here we will concentrate on places that inspire, inform and otherwise contribute to the formation of an architect.

In the formative first year of their studies it is critical that students are exposed to the good, bad and ugly reality of real places. Within the context of platforms such as social media, a lack of engagement with culture and impatience for shortcuts to success, influenced by how they were taught at school, there is a risk that new architecture students may not know how to look and listen to a place, site, or situation. It takes a huge effort to understand a place, so that they can then propose, design and build something there. As teachers we endeavour to remind students that the internet is a tool, a medium, not the world.

Architects have to understand a place, location or site, before making any act of intervention through building. The character of a place hugely depends upon its topography, history, politics, cultural framework, occupation, weather and setting. This understanding can only happen by personally experiencing the real place. In our first-year course it is a key mission to expose students as much as possible to this reality. This is achieved through taking them on study trips, walks, and through the year-one installation project, in which they look, listen, study, absorb, invent and finally propose and build a temporary design to 'adjust' a given place. Adjustment here means that the students establish a critical understanding of the existing place and work within its real and imagined qualities.

If places could write their memories, if those mnemonic demons could share their stories with us, if we could listen to their voices and remember, then we would appreciate their invisible lives upon which we need to build our future as architects. The meaning of a place comes from the act of inhabiting it and uncovering the layers of experience, events, and memories that it holds. In a culture obsessed with lens- and screen-based visual media, architects and students are often inclined to rely on a representation of a place to understand it. But, the experience of 'being there' is invaluable in places: it connects people at particular moments and situations embedded in the site-specific qualities of a place. It is that real experience that builds the meaning and the value of place in our minds, which then enables us as designers to interact. For an architect, this means gaining an understanding of the scale of a place compared to the human body; connecting to a place through the sense of smell, sound, humidity, darkness, light, silence, density, other occupants, materiality and weathering, its traces of history and invisible spirits. All this contributes to cultivating the architect's sensibility towards a place.

Character and value

FP: Being physically in a place offers up fragmented memories, the personal meanings we attach to experiences, as well as our intuitive and unpredictable ideas and feelings. This contributes to constructing a place in our minds that connects these ideas in a unique way, particular to a specific moment and situation. New, old and revisited places all connect in our eyes and minds. It is these frameworks of possible, ephemeral and hugely unpredictable and irrational connections that enrich our reading of a place.

Cultivating ways of looking and interpreting places is a primary mission in teaching first-year undergraduate architecture students. It is easy for a student to miss the pleasure of visiting and temporarily inhabiting a messy, dirty, muddy site, and studying the virtues, vices and pleasures of various interactions with it.

Developing a design for a particular place and situation is tough, and understanding is a very slow process. There is nothing more satisfying than designing a building that makes a place richer, and brings its hibernating qualities to the surface. The essence of a place – its magic, memories, sounds, smells, climate, connections, views, soil, whispers and fragmented memories – has to be personally understood, parallel to the pragmatic requirements that need to be accommodated at a particular location.

Looking and listening to a place with an open, fresh and inquisitive mind is critical. Once an architect, architecture student or apprentice understands the character, ideas, histories, stories, qualities and needs of a place, then comes the magic moment of gradually building up a relationship with the site, a dialogue that should have a clarity, vision and focus upon what matters in each situation or location; after this, one can build. There are times when the architect does nothing but reinforce certain qualities that are dormant, and sometimes the architect has to be daring and go radically against the current conditions and reality. A place is like a person: it has a personality and character. Often, one has to take it apart and, through design intervention, put the pieces back again in a very particular way.

Intuition, instinct and rationality, or in most cases a mixture of all, are important constituents in experiencing a place. In addition to this, architecture students need to be taught that places and buildings are meaningless, pointless and boring without human interaction. In a 2019 talk at The Bartlett, London-based architect and teacher, Peter Barber, stated 'it is only through its occupation that [a building] gets a meaning, it makes sense only through humans using it'.[5] It is a very particular attitude to regard a place or building as a backdrop to an occupation, activity or event. Certain key figures on the topic of how an architect can look at a place include Carlo Scarpa and Glenn Murcutt. Students are encouraged to take on Murcutt's message that 'understanding a place is 90 per cent of what you've got to achieve as an architect'.[6]

Myth and reality

JM: Places are always, literally, grounded in reality. They have geographical co-ordinates and physical characteristics. In some cases they might, through experience, memory and association, become intertwined with mythology, whether personal or as part of a broader culture. Places with these associations immediately become interesting as sites, because they invite students and tutors to think beyond the normal perceptual grounds of what can be seen or researched. This provides an analogical supporting structure that can unlock creative thoughts.

The relationship between place and mythology may lie more in anthropology than strictly historical research, though for the purposes of this book such academic distinctions are neither relevant nor helpful. There is a long tradition of relating place to mythology, which, as we shall see, is vital to Pimenides' concept of place.

London – much of which is a product of brutal, visceral, Anglo-Saxon capitalism – nonetheless has some imaginative interstices, fortunately so, because it is the base of Pimenides' teaching operations. Her discovery of London started with a mixture of distilled impressions. The first were centred around Marylebone, home of the Polytechnic of Central London, where she was a student, and her territory expanded with such experiences as a live project for a playground in Islington. London, she intuited, exuded a great deal of creative potential precisely because it was, in many areas, drab and run down, with vacant, underused, or unallocated sites.

Meanwhile, her appreciation of London's special characteristics grew. Personal impressions and experiences of different aspects and locations within the city merged with comments and insights from friends and colleagues. Pimenides recalls that Alvin Boyarsky, chair of the Architectural Association, where she taught in the late 1980s, claimed that London is not a

5. Peter Barber, The Bartlett International Lecture Series, 25 September 2019, The Bartlett, UCL.
6. Glenn Murcutt, Living Cities Forum, May 2019, Melbourne and Sydney.

2.2

2.3

2.4

European city in the conventional sense, as 'every day you turn a corner and you see something new'. London is a collage of little villages, each with its own character that can be represented, history that can be researched, and mythologies that can be imagined. London, Pimenides realised, was not primarily about monuments, but ordinary pieces of derelict urban fabric, undemonstrative but important social buildings like libraries, and greasy spoon cafés. This combination was fertile ground for nurturing her ideas about teaching.

Pimenides' adoption of London as a didactic tool coincides with her appointment at The Bartlett. Not surprisingly, her first detailed investigation of a piece of London in this manner was the campus of UCL itself. The programme she devised with her team called for a dramatic installation or performance somewhere outside, beyond the limits of the studio, that would last for a short time – hours or days at most – and to which guests from inside and outside The Bartlett would be invited.

At the end of the autumn term of 1990, 50 first-year students, led by their recently appointed team of tutors, entertained a number of guests including academics, writers, architects and teachers. Pimenides had asked the college authorities for support and found several locations in and around the university precinct: the grand UCL portico staircase, Senate House's high chamber, the archaeology department's terrace, a studio in Wates House, and the crypt of Gordon Square's Church of Christ the King. A different course of an elaborate feast was served in each location to slightly incredulous but intrigued guests, including myself. Each course had its own twist as well as its own location, and presented a locality most of the guests knew well in rather different ways. At the very least, it established the efficacy of moving out of the studio not just to select sites but to deliver the projects on them as well.

This 'feast' was the first of a long line of installations in different parts of London, which we examine further in chapter five. Many were within Sir John Soane's Museum or Pitzhanger Manor in Ealing, Soane's former country house. Others have been on the bank of the canal in Hackney or on one occasion taken the form of a spectacular procession from The Bartlett's temporary home in Hampstead Road back to reoccupy its long-term base at 22 Gordon Street, after it underwent major reconstruction.

These special, almost carnivalesque events, where conventions are deliberately and temporarily broken or suspended, show the familiar in an unfamiliar light. The intention is to interact with the nature of the place – physical and non-physical – through imaginative means. In this way, the installations imbue their sites with new layers of meaning but the underlying issue is how they gain that potential in the first place – what is it about London's history and fabric that make it so plentiful in number and richness of site?

The great semi-public spaces Sir John Soane designed in public institutions no longer exist, like the law courts clustered alongside Westminster Hall or the complex site and fabric of the Bank of England, so these installations used Pitzhanger Manor in Ealing and Sir John Soane's Museum in Lincoln's Inn Fields instead. Both are publicly accessible and extraordinarily suggestive in the sense of place they create. Pitzhanger has an intriguingly allusive façade, striking spaces and overlooks a magnificent public park. The museum is richer and denser in its architectural devices and allusions, and in the artfully displayed collection.

FP: Each of these locations provided fecund settings for teaching programmes over many years. A lot of exciting events and experiences in life depend on people and accidental encounters. One summer evening, in the early years of the 21st century, in search of some air I escaped to the garden in Gordon Square. Reclining on a grass mound and reading, I ended up chatting to the woman next to me. She was Jane Monaghan, later to become a beloved colleague and treasured friend. At the time we met she was in charge of all education programmes at Sir John Soane's Museum. Thanks to that escape to my local London square, I ended up volunteering to teach young people about architecture at the Soane Saturday Club; in parallel, Jane generously invited my students to the museum for a short tour. That was the start of a wonderful eight-year partnership between The Bartlett's year one and Soane's magical world. Lincoln's Inn Fields became the theme and teaching tool, and Soane's Pitzhanger Manor was the setting for our experimental installation projects. With a deep mutual trust and a generous spirit of collaboration, we were allowed to use Walpole Park, in which the house sits, as a testing ground for eight years of experiments in 'adjusting space', responding to themes inspired by Soane's domestic kingdom in Holborn. Those were great years spent interpreting Soane's stories, crafting wonderful furniture-scale pieces that inhabited Pitzhanger Manor, adjusting its spaces, and introducing eight cohorts of students to a magical world of collaboration, making, dream and reality.

Field trips

FP: The purpose of the field trip is twofold: on one hand it is for students to visit places and spend approximately a week of intense study where their projects might be located: they see and experience, hands-on, buildings, places and different cultures. It illustrates that in spite of studio culture and lectures, it is a most valuable eye-opener for an architect to be able to visit incredible places and buildings that you might be familiar with but have never experienced. Field trips can enable students to cultivate empathy and curiosity, to understand the value of various architectural qualities and ideas that matter, as well as form a personal and tactile connection with these places. They also provide an opportunity for collective living and bonding, and cultivate team spirit, all of which are invaluable to an architect's life and survival. The daily act of sharing a meal around a table with a small student group is a profound experience that teaches them how to communicate with each other, how to develop a point of view, how to enjoy disagreeing about ideas and have a beautiful moment of life-work together.

Trips are magical eye-openers to distinct cultures, alien worlds and what collective life is. In 2000, amongst the labyrinth of the tight Neapolitan backstreets, we were squeezed and embedded in a compact and multi-layered world with the smell of fresh, colourful fruit dancing in the air next to laundry drying on washing lines. The colours of the fresh vegetables and the crumbling baroque stonework provided a basis for the unique tapestry of life: flavours, smells, conversation, unfamiliarity and homeliness. The tight streets and the public squares were buzzing with vibrant life: scooters zooming along next to grandmothers reading stories and playing with youngsters on the steps of their houses. In contrast to these scenes, a series of spacious and serene public church interiors provided relief from the noisy and dense street life. Leaving the profane world of Naples and ascending onto the sacred slopes and peak of Mount Vesuvius felt like a once in a lifetime experience. The intimacy and awe that we felt right at the edge of a steaming volcano, seeing the expanse of the past empires, was humbling. To share this sublime experience with a small group of students was a deeply emotional experience.

To further illustrate the importance of 'being there' are three memorable moments of the visit to Italian Renaissance architect Andrea Palladio's 16th-century Villa Rotonda and Teatro Olimpico, and the main square in Vicenza, from a recent trip to Venice and Veneto. The entry path to Villa Rotonda is a well-known historical example, a pure and symmetrical building – I was astonished by its positioning in the landscape. Seeing it in its place is a totally unexpected experience for which everything one might have seen or heard about it is no preparation. The route between the garden gate and the villa itself, at the end of a gravel passage surrounded by two very tall garden walls, accentuates the distance. With statues that seem to look at visitors inquisitively lining the passage, the villa feels detached from the reality of the gate. Situated at the top of the a hill is a totally asymmetric building, the experience of the four façades is totally different to what one expects from looking at its architectural plans and photos, due to the light, shadow, view and weathering of the surrounding walls. The ceremonial route somehow disorientates you and cuts off the villa from the setting. When one ascends up to the porticos and looks back to where one came from, one experiences a very powerful connection to the distant horizon and Venetian landscape. This detachment from reality, which is still connected to the faraway parts of the landscape, for me, is the main quality of the villa.

Let us now consider another example, which is a complete reversal of the villa, the same architect's Teatro Olimpico. Externally, it is a modest building but it contains the most magical imaginary world. It is a theatre, but its backstage area becomes an ideal city of perspectival representation. The central stage is the first example in history of perspectival illusionary effects. Due to the slope of the ground and manipulations of scale, a huge street can be reconstructed backstage in a relatively short depth of space. It is a landscape where one's eyes and mind can wander.

The third example is the Piazza dei Signori in Vicenza, with Palladio's basilica on one side. This space undergoes a radical transformation, from a room inhabited by thousands of objects and people in a homely manner on market day to robust civic emptiness the rest of the week. With our students we would talk about the edges of that space, the emptiness, fullness and central occupation. In chapter four, we refer to the central study spaces and the edges as a teaching tool.

Sharing experiences during field trips is an absolutely vital ingredient needed in building students' appreciation of studio culture. I would like to refer to two moments during our field trips to Istanbul. In one, my co-director Patrick Weber carefully balanced himself on the roof of a *caravanserai* (roadside inn). In the second, I wedged myself in-between monolithic Byzantine city walls on the northwest of the city, experiencing, in reverse, what it is to conquer the city wall.

2.5

2.6

2.7

2.8

Another emotional and powerful moment was revisiting Peter Behrens' early 20th-century turbine factory in Berlin in January 2017, a few decades after I first saw it as a student. More than a hundred years after it was built, the power of its beautifully engineered and detailed epic cast iron columns is profound. For a first-year student, it is fundamental to see such a milestone building in its real context and touch and feel the tactile qualities and daunting power of those phenomenal columns. Studying and surveying those beautifully proportioned weathered beasts was almost a religious experience.

Understanding place: step-by-step

FP: It is both critical and fundamental to teach year-one students the appropriate means of recording and surveying their personal observations, as well as objective factual information. Traditional techniques, as well as experimental ones, are always valuable. Surveying, measuring, sketching, drawing both roughly and precisely, photographing, model making, writing poetry and daydreaming, are equally key to communicating information about site ideas and qualities. Intuition and empathy are vital to understanding a place.

The next stage is to interact, act upon, and design – wondering and wandering. The joy of designing within a given real place or site is the constant play between fiction and reality. Students are guided in how to respond to these requirements, and are shown the practical rules and skills of our trade. What is the context of a site? How immediate is it? How distant? Understanding context takes time: it is history, events, topography, finance, memory, politics, occupation, infrastructure, microclimate, light conditions, noise, density, scale, exposure and character. Sitting in a café patiently observing how the movement changes, light falls, sounds vary, life unfolds, how the pace of activities completely transforms the nature of a place, and how meaning is built up slowly though memory, inhabitation and connection to the place. Often various stories are discovered in parallel, they adapt to each other and all these ad-hoc fragments of information give meaning to a particular location. As architects we are privileged to be entrusted to intervene in a site. We have to find our own ways of looking at things, to interpret our readings of the site, and need to explore rational facts as well as trusting our instincts while spending time in a place.

This understanding and interpretation of the situation, condition and character of a site and its wider region should happen alongside designing a building, and be developed and refined daily while the architect progresses their design. Among many, there are several key architects and sites that we always refer students to, for their amazing abilities to interpret regions, places and sites. One of the most evocative examples is Carlo Scarpa's Querini Stampalia (1961–63) in Venice, Italy. Scarpa critically reinterpreted Venetian topography and history in relationship to the water and material sensibilities. The second example is Glenn Murcutt's Ball-Eastaway House (1982) in Sydney, Australia, which reflects his philosophy of responding to the views of a place, the spirit, air and topography, whilst considering what a wall or a window mean, and the relationship between the interiors and the immediate and distant places all around.

Since 1990, most of the sites for our main building project have been situated in London. There are multiple reasons why it is so useful and educationally beneficial to do so: it is a metropolis with a multiplicity of cultures, histories, grains, densities, characters and scales. There is an excitement of surprises. London used to have endless derelict buildings, sadly mostly gone as the whole city is racing into (often pointless) development. The encounter with derelict fragments of the past is invaluable for many reasons: it reveals parts of interior spaces and elements that are normally hidden. These tangible, tactile, fragments of past lives constitute an invaluable world of reference for freshly initiated architecture students who are able to see ways of construction, weathering of materials and characters of different hidden lifestyles. The interiors – fragmented, open to interpretation, exposed – become notional scaffolding, framework and backdrop that can be used, or not, in many different ways. The layered fragments become excellent storytellers and feed a young student's imagination with limitless imagined worlds. Gaps in street frontages, and dereliction, avoid the myth of perfection and invite intervention. We discuss some of the projects we have created in these spaces in chapter five.

Among other numerous benefits of using locations within the urban fabric of the city is the availability of so many different scales and characters of surrounding boundaries. It is a canvas of different periods of development, an amazing living library of life for construction, occupation and materiality, making all sorts of cultural meanings. These qualities make it a great testing ground for a student's first attempt to produce a building. Such places can be the best teachers for a student to understand ideas and qualities of boundaries, threshold, density, scale, orientation, and the back and front of a building. Further invaluable lessons can be learned from studying and understanding a street, a public square or courtyard, the profound importance of the ground level of a building and how its sits on the ground,

2.9

2.10

2.11

2.12

73

the potential, duty, and key role of a façade, or a public rooftop. How do private and public life meet: At the façade? At a doorway?

Above all, to understand a place – a site that one plans to design and build something on – takes time. It takes drawing, thinking, measuring, redrawing, revisiting a place and trusting your intuition and critical mind to take the right decisions, for all sorts of parameters. For a first-year student, it is crucial to get a taste of this magic trilogy: the mind and the hand of the architect, doodling at a drawing board or in the mud whilst experiencing the smell and sound of a real site; the builder or craftsman intimately inhabiting and bonding with a site through building; and people occupying a built structure or object, transforming it, giving it meaning in other ways.

At the same time, the fresh mind of a student needs also to be daring, often silly, having fun and making bold mistakes. There is nothing more useful than 'being within' a place, visiting and revisiting it over the years. At The Bartlett, the fabric of London has assisted us hugely and we love it for that.

JM: From the foregoing it is obvious that, for Pimenides, the idea of place has great value in architectural education. Architecture has to work with context, and at least for teaching purposes, the richer and more allusive that context the better. A skilful design will take whatever programmatic requirements a brief has and find ways of accommodating them within a given site – and, in live examples, taking account of cost and other practicalities – but in doing so, will interact with and possibly modify whatever activities take place nearby. On some occasions this interaction can reach a level of intensity where all those activities enter into a relationship in which they can adapt and change around each other, leading to a different balance in the area, and transforming its social, spatial and economic dynamic.

This sort of mutation need not be confined to the everyday, functional level. With Pimenides' belief that sites have mythological and allegorical significance, as well as physical conditions, the interaction can invite exchange between different times and allegory, metaphor and reality. In this sense, a well-chosen site and a well-considered project brief can become a microcosm of the cultural dynamic, which is the essence of what she thinks students should take away from architectural education. In this sense, the sort of reading of 'place' that she found in her grandfather's garden at Ekali, outside Athens (see p. 76), is related to the sites on which she sets design projects, though in any outward sense they are poles apart. There is also a strong relationship with 'studio culture': if studio culture is the machine, then the proposals students make for their sites are the outcome – and once complete become a rung on their educational ladders.

Another important point in selecting places for project sites is scale. These sites are necessarily tiny elements within the whole city, and they must be appropriately sized for students to comprehend, but more importantly, appropriately sized within their immediate context, able to influence but not dominate it. Scale is, in other words, an element of the site and the project, which is interwoven with other physical and metaphorical strands.

Over three decades, Pimenides has chosen numerous sites for student projects in various parts of London. Different colleagues have influenced those choices, some having an affinity for reality, the physical grain and history, while others are less interested in the qualities sites have. Locations have included Spitalfields, for its variety and swings of fortune over the course of time, which leave traces; a series of sites in Camden, which together skeletally map its social as well as physical history; and for 2019, the Isle of Dogs. Over the decades The Bartlett has been using London as a teaching tool, the city's nature has changed. There are fewer derelict sites, and localities with unlikely but synergetic combinations of activities have also largely disappeared. The real living nature of the urban fabric, has in the process of economic development become more monocultural and so less capable of offering the tentative invitations to imagine that are important to Pimenides' teaching practice. The Isle of Dogs has a fascinating and mixed history, a place of massive engineering works, which gave birth to modern shipbuilding, as well as a place where pirates were hanged along its extensive shoreline. It abounds in history, but precious little physical grain has survived to give students something to appreciate with their own senses.

The following seven locations are critical for Pimenides. Each of them delivers a different interpretation of the value or reading of a place and how it relates to the process of design, meaning and occupation.

1. Ekali House, Mount Penteli, Greece

FP: Athens is my hometown, but the most visceral and informative 'place' I experienced with my family is in an area outside of the city. In the 1950s it was more or less a virgin site, though it is now a popular retreat from the city. My maternal grandfather Nikos Manthos, a professor of chemistry with a romantic streak, believed in the symbolic or allegorical significance of Greek mythology, despite his scientific training and profession. Taking me to Delphi, he imbued me with an interwoven fabric of topography, geology and mythology.

2.13

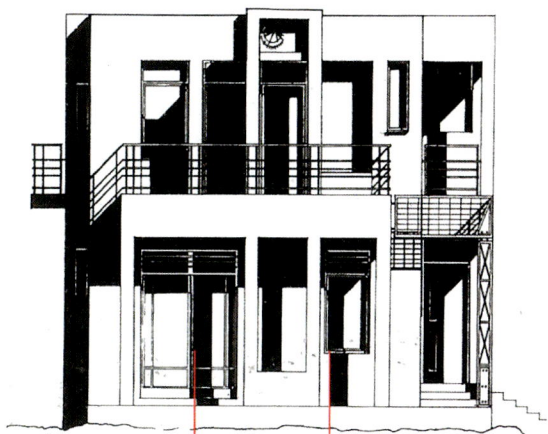

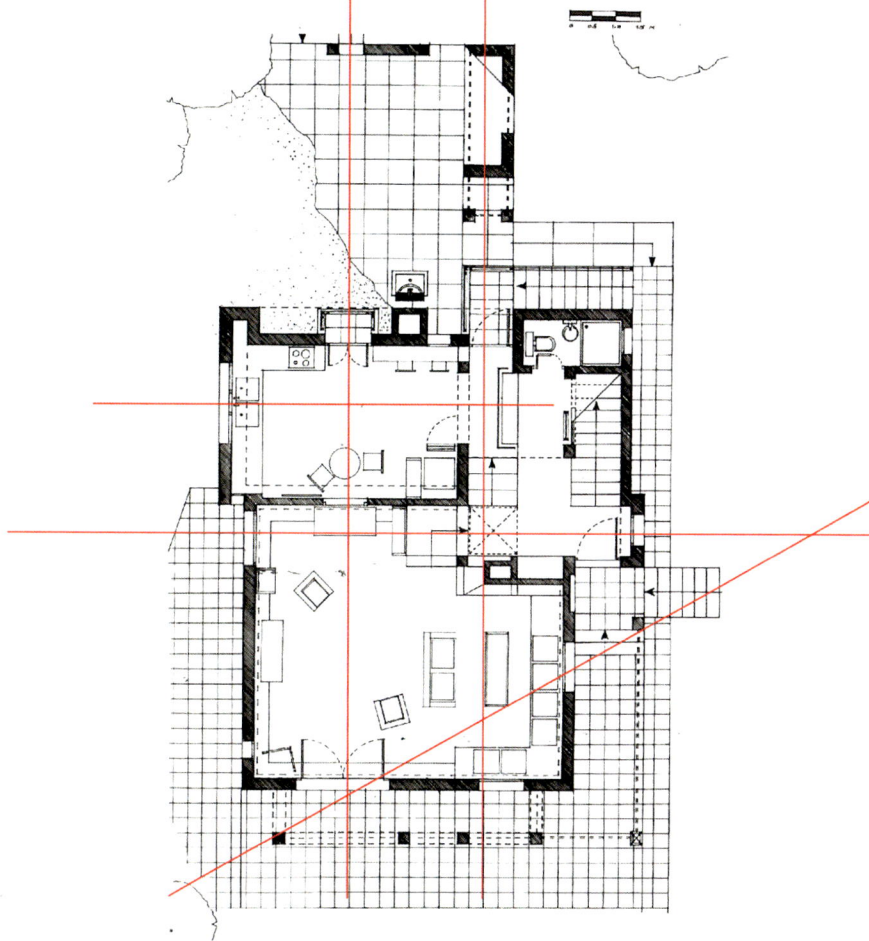

2.15

2.16

2.17

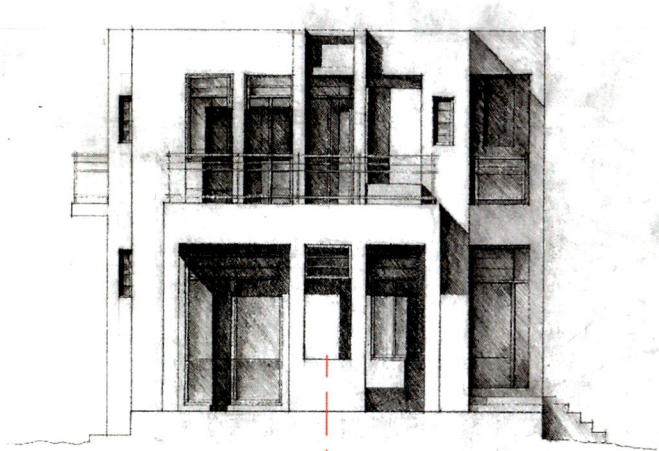

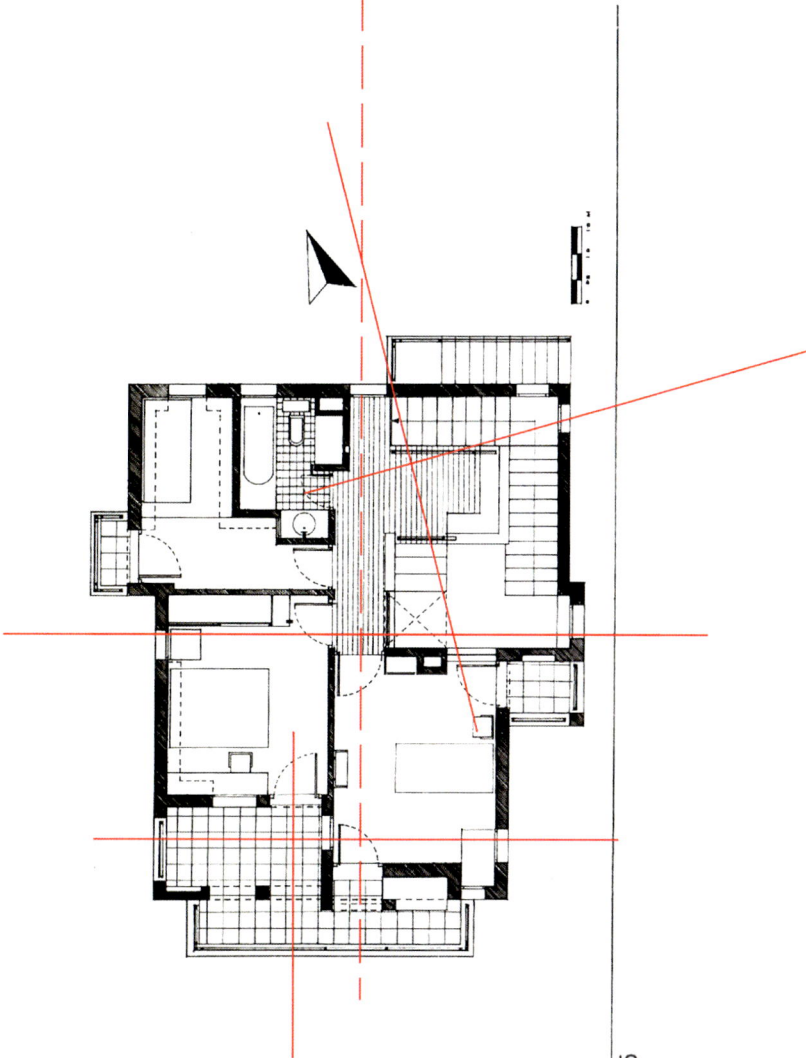

When he acquired a piece of land, he brought in shepherds from his home district of Epiros to begin to develop it. They brought plants and building traditions from Epiros, so the site was not just changing superficially but was also acquiring different cultural traces. Manthos continued the layering of traditions, with a stone building built in the vernacular of Epiros: a round Byzantine-inspired structure with various ancillary accommodations. One sleeping space was in a treehouse, others were decorated with his paintings of Knossos.

The area was called Ekali, after Ekalini, a girlfriend of Dionysius, the god of harvest and fertility. Here, time had no fixed chronology, and impressions of place were not tied to physical geography. Each element brought something different and complementary to the whole. Of its pursuit of pleasure, Dionysius himself would have approved. For me, the idea that that places could be hugely enhanced by having their own mythologies was significant.

Amongst milestone events of my childhood are memories of how a thousand pine cones and a stuffed eagle formed the roof of a garden pavilion; the ground of the old patio was overlaid with frescoes depicting Homeric travels; and goats' bells, from various regions of Greece, were embedded in all sorts of gates. The epitome of my childhood escape was helping Manthos build a stone fountain in the shape of a lion's head at the centrepiece of a miniature village consisting of a water mill, a donkey's stable, a two-storey doll's house and a pond for turtles. Those memories inspired me later in life when, as an architect, I had to understand what that place was. The immediate and surrounding location and context of its footprint bears witness to a childhood life embedded in and surrounded by the great storytelling and activities of my grandfather; this gave me a variety of rules upon which the first design concepts started.

Alsyion Effrosyni – as my grandfather named the garden – is the clearest example of how a place should inspire and guide the spirit and soul of a building. It is the site of the first project I designed and built, and it evokes memories every time I revisit it. I was commissioned during my diploma course, but the building took two years to design while I was a student, and eight months to build; a year after completion, it took six months to decide upon the colour applied to some key walls. A dialogue with certain family memories about particular spots of the surrounding land was critical. Viewing axes situated the main rooms, and the proportions of the openings provided a reference and affinity to the neoclassical tradition of Athenian dwellings.

This relatively small house is situated at the back of a garden, behind overgrown trees that separate the south (main) façade from the street. The house itself consists of eight distinct rooms organised horizontally and vertically around a two-storey-high entrance hall situated in the northeast part of the building. The orthogonal organisation of the house, emphasised by the clearly defined visual axes, represents its basic topography and orientation and is visible not only in the entrance hall but also in the perimeter. This primary order is complemented by the radial arrangement of the internal spaces, more specifically through the asymmetrical arrangement of the staircases leading from the entrance hall into the main living room, kitchen and upper floor. The radial arrangement of the rooms and their relationships with the internal atrium directly reflect their purpose and the daily life of the house. One typical example is the terrace on the upper floor in the interior of the atrium (void), which is used as a sitting area and mediating space between a fairly public ground floor and the private domain of the upper floor.

I wanted the house to refer to the traditional Attica dwelling. I decided to address this through the strictly vertical proportions of all openings and an initial symmetry reflected in the plan and elevation, which was gradually distorted due to the particularities of occupation, orientation and visual axes to particular points on the horizon. A passion for the local trees, stones, bushes and animals gave me the rule of not disturbing their positions; that restricted the footprint of the house to a 7 x 10-metre rectangle. This pure volume gradually became eroded and distorted, responding to other rules I decided to follow; explorations resulted in most external walls being pulled out, squashed and shifted to respond to views, the paths of the sunlight, and the weather.

The situation and the anchoring of the house directly refer to the timber treehouse-type pavilion that my grandfather himself had previously built on that particular spot. He painted the external elevations of the former pavilion with Minoan-style figures, adorning all four hardboard and stone elevations, paying homage to his favourite myths. Apart from the necessity and desire to connect internal and external inhabitation, the fenestration of the four façades of the new building visually connect particular garden locations that remind me of key events that had taken place during my childhood. The two main visual axes, which connect the distant landscape to the interior, intersect at a point that locates the only skylight of the dwelling. On the summer solstice, the moon becomes a lantern, lighting up the void at the entrance to the house. A sundial is positioned on the south façade, referring to the virtues and vices of the sun's path; a precious point, as the house is surrounded by a thick forest of annoying pine trees.

A constant dialogue between the occupation of the house in the various seasons, and day and night, is reflected in the organisation and concept of what a façade is. It is a deep space in which the following activities take place: various types of entrance; shading from the sun; protection from the elements; windowsill space where one can rest, write or gaze upon the distant landscape; sofa-benches for resting while looking at particular trees; a fireplace; storage; and external and internal sitting possibilities. All of these services are embedded within thick external walls. The character of the north, south, east and west façades is determined by the four very different qualities of the garden areas adjacent to them, with a huge variety of density, exposure, ground condition and view. The use of colour – the deep reds and blues alluding to Minoan frescoes and the lighter colours used to manipulate light – accentuates the depth of the key elevations of the house and clarifies the foreground and background positioning.

2. Acropolis, Athens

FP: The Acropolis is often referred to as a rock, an object, dropped in the middle of the city of Athens with hundreds of historically loaded interpretations. Le Corbusier's sketches of the Acropolis seen from a distance and his studies of Dimitris Pikionis' reconstruction of the Panathenaic route are a great example of someone spending intensive time looking, thinking, sketching and understanding the fragments that represent the essence of that place. His sketches are not descriptive but are profound diagrams that try to capture the essence of history, the place itself and his reading of that location. They illustrate a thought and an idea, and talk about topography, light, shadow, orientation and detailing.

The processional journey up the hill accentuates the physical distance between the profane city and the sacred rock; Pikionis' mosaic masterpiece, created in the 1950s, is a synthesis of new pieces of in-situ poured concrete and Byzantine and ancient fragmented relics, used as a language to reinstate the Panathenaic route. From the city around, it looks like a dominating object. Once you ascend up above, on the sacred rock, the reverse occurs: the gleaming fragmented ground condition is part of the grain of the city and the tops of buildings merge with eroded, shiny, fragmented rock surfaces. Every single piece of rock found on the plateau becomes a continuation of the cityscape, levelled with the rooftops of the buildings beneath. Visually, the edges of the Acropolis rock dissolve and a very powerful intimacy with the distant urban horizon emerges. The temples are no longer objects, they become the backdrop and the focus is the city beneath: the shiny, worn landscape of the rocky ground merging with the modern city. This moment is exemplified at the gateway, or *propylaia*, the point where the ancient Panathenaic route paused. The geometry, topography and dialectic between tactile and urban scale is phenomenal.

3. Meteora, Central Greece

FP: A rare geological phenomenon, the topography of Meteora is unique in the sense that right next to an ordinary country village you find stone formations at a prehistoric scale, in a surreal juxtaposition of the sacred with profane daily normality. The rocks' plateaus are inhabited by monasteries. Slowly leaving the secular world you ascend to these isolated religious precincts, gradually realising the power of the elements, wind, rain, darkness, and glare. You try to go up the steps hewn into the slippery rock and the rain pushes you down. The strength and proximity of this bodily exposure, the serene isolation, the dramatic topography and the monks' daily routines make this weirdly intimate Byzantine world a totally surreal normality.

The landscape is a constant play of distance and closeness. Stones, sky, darkness, light, ground, water and height all constantly mingle, creating a kind of orchestral performance, a simulating of a thousand parallel voices and instruments, with no sound. The proximity of the ground, the texture, the danger, travelling in and out of rocky caves, paths overlooking extreme sheer drops, and the constant interplay of being within a natural or artificial built form, make it a surreal but yet very familiar experience. Arriving after a long journey, you are rewarded by these spectacular Byzantine interiors, rarely seen in such an untouched manner. The entire openness of the landscape is totally opposed to the interiors of divine and sculpted darkness. The landscape of rock formations gives the feeling of being in a vast interior of very distant boundaries. The proximity of highly cultivated interior spaces wedged in-between these monolithic rocks can only be fully understood once one is embedded in that setting.

4. Delphi, Greece

FP: The ancient sanctuary is a civic public place, yet it allows a very intimate connection with the surrounding dramatic topography. The human viewer

2.19

2.20

2.21

2.22

2.23

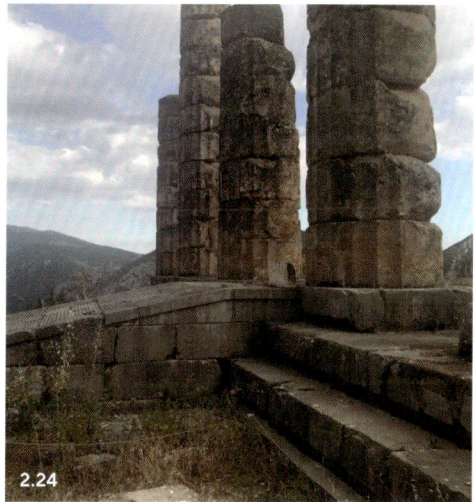

2.24

feels small and insignificant, in awe of the surroundings: stones, exposure to elements, weather, memories and thoughts. The topography and placing in the landscape of the whole sanctuary and all the temples in Delphi is the strongest example of the presence of the ancient gods. Fragments of all scales are scattered yet highly organised remnants of times past. The light, the scale, the cavity of the mountains and the precise positioning of the Temple of Apollo, the Oracle of Pythia, within a crack between two mountains, all create a blur between upper, lower, chthonic, real, and imagined. The dramatic landscape, the extreme vertical topography of the mountains within which the sanctuary is placed in contrast to the scale of the human body, the exposure to the distant landscape, the sky, and the changeability of the weather all contribute to a very profound feeling of fear and awe.

5. Houdetsi, Labyrinth Centre of Musical Workshops, Crete

FP: Southeast of Knossos in Crete is Mount Juktas, 800 metres above sea level. A mountain of enormous significance in Minoan prehistoric civilisation, it is believed to be the place of Zeus' burial tomb and is a site where early human sacrifice is thought to have taken place. Juktas proudly acts as a topographical backdrop, as an elder anchor and reference to all the places around it. It is in this powerful setting that the humble and remote village of Houdetsi is situated, where the philosopher, educator and visionary musician Ross Daly founded the Labyrinth Musical Workshop, 30 years ago. Situated in a restored manor house with a large garden, its main role is a 'meeting point for outstanding world musicians and students from all over the world, a leading force with respect to education, collaboration amongst various cultures in the field of modal and traditional music'.[7]

For a number of years, on the first weekend of August, the three-day Houdetsi Music Festival took place, which transformed the quiet Cretan mountain village into a cultural event, where sounds reverberated across the whole of the Mediterranean and beyond. Hundreds of top-class musicians would perform for free, thousands of visitors would come from all over the world to listen, participate, teach, meet and debate, and locals would sell their homemade delicacies on carefully laid tables in the narrow streets. Locals, visitors and musicians would sing, dance, eat and drink together until dawn. Hundreds of volunteers, who believed in Daly's vision of changing the world

---

7. Labyrinth Musical Workshop, www.labyrinthmusic.gr/en/home, accessed 27 August 2021.

through music, would come from neighbouring municipalities to manage the huge crowds flooding the village. There would be a multiplicity of parallel music performances in the various squares, wide streets, churchyards and gardens, and as they were scattered around the village, the echoes of these divine instruments and voices would transport participants to a dream world. It was as if the spirit of Zeus, from the heights of Juktas' slopes, was conversing with them in a strangely profound and immediate way. The sounds would flood the otherwise quiet and humble village and the ground would vibrate, creating a sensation that the place itself was an active member of the festival. How was it possible that, in that plethora of people, animals, children, instruments, cars and food consumption, there was no crime, theft or rubbish flooding the streets? Well beyond Labyrinth's own agendas, this event enabled many adjacent villages to promote and sell their exquisite homemade delicacies and farm produce, enabled musicians to network and local shops to flourish.

If we refer to Simon Sinek's theory of leadership,[8] Ross Daly is the epitome of a leader who inspires, who enthuses people with his vision, talent and generosity, making them believe in and trust him. As with Sinek's description of leadership, he does not give orders and instructions of the 'what and the how', his collaborators believe in his vision that 'Labyrinth is more than a musical workshop, it is a way of life through music'.[9] In turn, he trusts people and gives them the opportunity to achieve their best: a true embodiment of a collective culture, of exchange, of mutual trust and support.

All of the above illustrates clearly that places and buildings acquire meaning from human activity and occupation. During the festival, over the period of a few hours, a set of quiet neighbourhoods were transformed into a web of interconnected 'rooms' through the sounds of the lyra, oud, violin, tambur, and the performance of players and participating public. The village's humble and derelict pathways were transformed into lavish sophisticated 'interiors', alluding to distant lives of a Minoan era, a rich interwoven alchemy of sound, music, whispers and smells of freshly baked Cretan delicacies, transforming that modest setting into a rich and sophisticated lived space. The headquarters – the brain, soul and spirit of Labyrinth – is housed within this serene domestic world, in the old stone and timber manor house. Its large garden in front is a paradise for Daly's many rescue dogs, and in a wonderful walled garden, lessons, orchestral practices, experimental playing and

8. Sinek is discussed further in chapter 1, pp. 52–53.
9. Labyrinth Musical Workshop, www.labyrinthmusic.gr/en/home, accessed 27 August 2021.

2.25

2.26

2.27

2.28

2.29

2.30

musical exchanges take place. The manor's large interior spaces are filled with a wonderful museum collection of traditional instruments that students are able to use. During the day, the grounds of the Labyrinth headquarters serve as the kingdom of those beloved dogs and as a music practice room open to all students. At night, during the festival, the dramatically lit façade acted as the backdrop to powerful orchestral performances. The local family-run café opposite Labyrinth, another anchor to the transitory musicians, was equally transformed: during the day it would act as a home in transit, a large courtyard-living room, study and networking place; by night it would become the most active, jazzy, loud, fun and social place imaginable.

6. Sydney Opera House, Australia

FP: Flying over the southeastern Australian landscape is a profound and emotional experience. There is deep pleasure in seeing those beautiful land formations from above, the volcanic topography and the scooped out, eroded, red land. This poses a key question for me: How can a young student, an architect, understand how to build, if one does not study the land itself? Here, I found it more powerful than anywhere I had seen before.

Visiting Jørn Utzon's masterpiece, completed in 1973, was probably one of the most shocking architectural experiences of my life. The real qualities of the Sydney Opera House are completely missed and distorted by its shallow pictorial representations through photography: its scale, crucial relationship to the city and harbour, and the life it holds within, around and far beyond. Visiting the site revealed the merits of 'being there', in several specific ways:

1.   The Opera House is at the meeting point of the Botanical Gardens, the high-rise financial district and the bay of Sydney Harbour. Its exact location is a place of profound historical significance; its history refers to the meeting point of the water and the Aboriginal Elders.

2.   It is situated at the end of a route and gives a strong feeling that it is 'holding' the city. Descending down the hill, one is bound on the left by the tall cityscape and in front lies a green carpet, the magical Botanical Gardens, inhabited by a huge range of trees with gigantic strange old roots. Slowly the familiar white sails of the Opera House emerge on the horizon, embedded in a visual jungle of treetops, boats, bridges, sky, clouds, seagulls, sea, trains, cars and all sorts of distant sounds. The juxtaposition of the extremes – the dense area of high-rise towers,

the idyllic bay and huge root-monsters – provides a unique, unfolding approach to the Opera House. The gardens suddenly stop and are held back by a robust monolithic stone wall. Immediately below, the stone paved forecourt of the Opera House commences, which then slowly becomes a tectonic mound of highly accentuated steps. This dramatic ascending structure artificially reinstates the natural topography of the gardens next door. That dramatic stepped concrete mound terminates in the Opera Bar, where it forms a gigantic, cantilevered windowsill, celebrating the entry.

3.   An extraordinary similarity between the bundled-up gigantic botanical roots and the fan-like concrete supernatural columns makes one wonder. The building interprets and reinstates the surreal roots in the most robust, yet elegant manner. The robust yet tactile scale, together with the finesse and thoughtful fragility of the concrete and timber details, reveals Utzon's genius.

4.   All pictorial representations of this building, alluding to sails, seagulls, etc., arguably ignore its most important aspects. For me, these are the building's location, its profound and careful interpretation of the history and topography, the various inhabitations and uses, its relation to the bay, the city, the local and transit activities surrounding it, the difference between the spatial qualities and events of day and night, and how it becomes an anchor and reference point for the whole city. All those gestures, in that particular place, make it an architectural masterpiece. Being within that place, looking out onto Sydney's bay, back to the gardens and the city, one appreciates how this single item is holding together the adjacent topography, as well as being generated by it. It is the meeting point of people and waters, the essence of the spirit of Sydney, a special 'togetherness'.

5.   Finally, the division between interior and exterior is a celebration of well-orchestrated architectural moves: glass, concrete, timber, views, seagulls perched next to well-dressed cocktail drinkers; amazing views to all the four different scenes surrounding the building and ceremonially ascending dramatic stairs all create parallel and multiple polyphonies of life. Like a protective cocoon, these spaces engulf the huge internal concert hall itself. A space completely cut off, it is an anticlimax to the plethora of the various foyers, galleries, terraces and paths surrounding it.

The brief for the Sydney Opera House was vague, asking for a place for gathering and experimental performances.[10] The place, as built and used at present, holds a huge range of activities. Day and night conditions are totally different and encourage a variety of uses that do not rely on commercial enterprises but on the architectural structure of the place that enables and encourages people to inhabit it. This allows for more spontaneous occupation of the surrounding spaces. The ambiguity of the threshold between interior and exterior enables and inspires all sorts of occupation. It is a beautiful orchestration of urban life, topography and music.

7. The Lake Room, Sydney National Park, Australia

FP: In the jungle of the southern Sydney National Park, descending through the dense weird and wild vegetation and hilly terrain, one arrives unexpectedly at a clearing. The approach through the jungle to this place is an uncomfortable journey, where the body comes into close contact with horrible aggressive bushes, slippery stone hills, a huge range of nasty insects and deep overshadowed passages. It is a dramatic journey that suddenly brings you out of the blue into an open space in the forest. It is the meeting point of several springs that form a seemingly bottomless lake that perfectly reflects its counter in a surreal reversal of gravity. This mirrored body is roughly 30 x 60 metres and is bound to a vertical forest soaring to the heavens. It feels like a complete enclosure whose walls are made of a thick forest of trees and vegetation. The floor is a combination of dirt, insects crawling, little seeds and large tectonic sheets of flat boulders with slippery moss sunbathing on the rocky outcrops. The most surreal quality is the way the evening light makes human shadows rise to a scarily gigantic scale as if they are trying to meet you. It is a space as untouched by humans as one could possibly imagine. Listening to the silence, with the occasional squawk of a bird flying through, is a completely surreal experience. The lengthy journey, the vast scale of this site, and its distinctive serenity make it a profoundly lonely and, for some, spiritual location. The slippery ground, the fear of insects, the quick falling of dusk, and the loss of sense of time, all accentuate its distance from normality and reality.

---

10. See Peter Murray, *The Saga of Sydney Opera House*, Routledge, 2003, especially pp. 1-11, which recounts the circumstances of how the Sydney Opera House originated.

2.31

2.32

2.33

Chapter 2 images

Photographs courtesy of Frosso Pimenides unless otherwise stated.

2.1 Forum Romanum, year-one field trip, January 2019.

2.2 Sir John Soane's Museum, a place where, for several successive years, Pimenides says year-one staff and students 'wandered, discovered, made friends, and were inspired to "adjust" other spaces'. Photo courtesy of Sir John Soane's Museum.

2.3 The River Thames from City Hall. Celebrating the 25th anniversary of Open City (Open House), with founder Victoria Thornton and the Mayor of London, Sadiq Khan, 14 September 2017.

2.4 Frosso Pimenides' working sketch for Butler's Wharf development, Conran Roche Architects, London, 1988.

2.5 Tall ships by Tower Bridge, London, Golden Jubilee, 2002.

2.6 The preserved, ruined, façade at Butler's Wharf that became the reference and starting point of the mixed-development project (see 2.4).

2.7 Digital collage by year-one student, field trip to Naples, 2001. Photo: Architecture BSc year-one archive.

2.8 Visit to the top of steaming Vesuvius. Year-one field trip to Naples, 2001.

2.9 The main square and Andrea Palladio's Basilica, year-one field trip to Vicenza, 2019.

2.10 Teatro Olimpico by Palladio, year-one field trip to Vicenza, 2019.

2.11 Column detail at Peter Behrens' AEG factory, Berlin, 2018.

2.12 Fountain detail, Piazza Navona. Year-one field trip to Rome, 2020.

2.13 Family house at Ekali, designed, drawn, and construction supervised by Frosso Pimenides, Mount Penteli, Ekali, Athens, 1983-86. Photo: Dimitris Kalapodas.

2.14 Frosso Pimenides' grandfather and mentor Nikos Manthos, Eagle Kitchen Hut at Ekali, 1955. Photo: George Pimenides.

2.15 Frosso Pimenides, south elevation and ground floor plan for the new house at Ekali, hand drawings in ink; red lines mark the visual axes that locate the interior spaces and the openings' relationship to the place.

2.16 The entry space at the new house at Ekali, 1985. Photo: Dimitris Kalapodas.

2.17 The old house at Ekali, with frescoes painted by Pimenides' grandfather Nikos Manthos, inspired by those at Knossos.

2.18 Frosso Pimenides, first-floor plan for the new house at Ekali, hand drawn in ink, and south elevation in pencil; study no.14, exploring proportions and the depth of the façade.

2.19 Acropolis, detail of Dimitris Pikonis' Panathenaic pathway up to the rock, Athens.

2.20 Acropolis, the surface of the rock visually extending into the Athens cityscape, June 2017.

2.21 Propylaia, Acropolis, looking back towards the city, Athens, June 2017.

2.22 Meteora in central Greece, with monasteries dating from as early as 11th century CE built on rock formations, December 2018.

2.23 & 2.24 Delphi, June 2017.

2.25 Shadows at sunset in the bush, Sydney National Park, 17 February 2017.

2.26 The lake room in the bush, Sydney National Park, 17 February 2017.

2.27 Tree roots in the Royal Botanic Garden, Sydney, close to Sydney Opera House, February 2017.

2.28 The upper part of Sydney Opera House foyer, described by Pimenides as 'a magical space where the city and the surrounding topography gradually enter and address the interior'. For her it is 'the most powerful, poetic, inventive use of in-situ concrete'. Architect: Jørn Utzon, completed 1973. Photographed in February 2017.

2.29 The undercroft of the grand entrance stairwell of Sydney Opera House, February 2017.

2.30 Detail, Sydney Opera House, 2017.

2.31 Performance at the home of Labyrinth Musical Workshop in Crete, launched in 1982 by Ross Daly, August 2019.

2.32 Musician wandering on the Cretan mountains, 2020.

2.33 Pantheon, Rome, January 2020. Pimenides observes: 'People and places, real and imagined, are all in a powerful dialogue with each other'.

Chapter 3: Fragments

The rooms

JEREMY MELVIN: Throughout her career at The Bartlett, the rooms Frosso Pimenides has occupied have played a central part in her teaching practice. They have been part sanctuary for colleagues and students, and part nerve centre for managing the teaching programme. Above all, they have been marked by a proliferating and changing collection of fragments – of buildings, projects, even of lives – that have played a central role in how she teaches. In this chapter we discuss how she began to use fragments and the implications that flow from doing so.

FROSSO PIMENIDES: Over the years, my offices in the various Bartlett buildings have been an anchor and reference point, and an annex to our Architecture BSc year-one teaching studios. There has often been a sense of complexity and fragility to the year-one world – after all, a group of young people taking their first steps in a new architectural adventure is always pioneering – and this office has often been vital to keeping things working well in our operations. Its value is as a meditative and intimate space, yet one that can be transformed to accommodate a range of collective or public situations. It is a room that all our staff and students can use. For me, it is a space in which I can wander in my daydreams, a place where I can discover endless exciting stories from my students, and where I have carried out so many tutorials that inspired me and gave me the enthusiasm to explore together with my students.

On a practical level, this office developed out of the daily need to store the necessary teaching materials used by students in our experiments, a place for weird stuff that we could share, and an ongoing collection of wonderfully inspiring models. Without planning, it spontaneously developed into a place to keep valuable, ad-hoc and insignificant yet inspiring fragments, from all sorts of epochs and places, as well as memorabilia that made the coexistence of past lives and future explorations possible.

It is also full of stuff, some precious, others borderline garbage but full of memories: wonderfully inspiring student work and models; stones picked up on field trips; photographs; maps; and personal relics collected over years of wandering. In between all these elements the visitor can escape from reality, dream, imagine, and curiously observe in a safe and private space. It is a collection of pieces from other places, times, and people. It is the latent power of all these collected and stored fragments that make those mental wanderings possible. As we will see in chapter four, the office serves as a centre of gravity and a retreat for both group and individual activities.

A very particular photograph (p. 96) of my last office in the old Wates House – room 327 – captures, for me, the essence and magic of a fragment, of wandering and wondering. The photograph, taken at dusk in late May 2014, epitomises my understanding of the idea of a 'memory theatre' as reference point and inspiration for design, teaching and research. The light entered the room from the west on that summer evening. The painful and exhausting packing of 120 crates was just about to commence as we prepared to relocate to our temporary building on Hampstead Road. The room accommodated a number of totally unrelated fragments of culture, life, teaching, work and research; personal as well as collective pieces of various academic lives. The room had served as an interview room for hundreds of applicants who, for 15 minutes, were able to share and taste what an architecture school might look and feel like. It served as a retreat for students and staff who, for a few moments, needed an escape from the dense world of production and duty that is inevitable in an architecture school. This sense of retreat and temporary dwelling was invaluable to all of us and, above all, to the main occupant: myself.

The dusty layers and stacks of carefully archived piles of unrelated fragments allowed occupants to connect in endless ways, giving a feeling of belonging and connection; similar to how a conductor might have a moment with certain instruments in the sea of his orchestra. This freedom of choice to connect in a meaningful way to all sorts of fragments, from all different types of classifications, times and backgrounds, enabled a series of personally meaningful dialogues between the student or visitor and the pieces themselves. Beyond the obvious role of demonstrating ideas, model-making skills and designs of past generations of students, a lot of these – mostly battered and fragmented, incomplete and ambiguous models – enabled the students' minds to wander and imagine other worlds, well beyond the tactile, crafted, material physicality of the model itself.

This office, as a physical place, was cut off from the rest of the studios, their culture and life through the magic of closing a door, fragmenting it from public life and teaching. This is what enables it to become a retreat and a haven. It is astonishing that a lowly door, covered with posters, hats and coats could fundamentally isolate or unite two entirely different worlds. Through the transformative power of this door, it becomes a fragment of my life, of my teaching, closely interwoven yet separate from the rest of the studios. The office, as it appears in this particular photograph, is made out of fragments of light that create a site-specific mosaic of objects. The office was the location of key milestone events, like initiating and planning the Accelerate outreach programme at UCL.[1] It was also a networking space for past and present heads of school and a place for informal conversations with teaching colleagues.

Amongst the collection of all sorts of unrelated pieces in that room there were also some fragments that capture certain key moments of my life, as reference points and sources of inspiration: an early Victorian bishop's pew containing an original chamber pot, used as model storage; photographs from my travels over the years; posters from milestone events and exhibitions I had visited; a large hand-painted wooden toybox housing documents and emergency clothing for site visits; my son's first first desk, adorned with childhood graffiti and positioned upside down, served as a perfect cabinet of curiosities that hosted an array of old student models; and above a sketch by my school friend Athanasios Spanomarides, capturing the life of a desolate urban square – a masterpiece of spontaneity, draughtsmanship, and profound symbolism.

On the walls, right up to the ceiling, were complete and fragmented lightweight models of a range of scales and material types, which served as an invaluable reference to making techniques and building models. To the left, the north wall hosted a dense juxtaposition of objects: a huge collection of plaster casts of students' hands, fruit, parts of buildings, dental features and city maps. Above it was a beautifully layered surreal collage (image 2.7, p. 69) of street scenes taken on a field trip to Naples back in 2001, an early example of digital documentation of a place. In transcending the actual reality, the work communicated the essence of what Naples meant to the author, a year-one student in 2000–2001. Next to it was a dusty, white, layered model of a Welsh mountain made from beer mats; apart from its robust longevity,

---

1. Accelerate is a design education and mentoring programme aimed at increasing diversity in the built environment professions. It was developed and established by Open City in partnership with The Bartlett. Every year, the programme provides 30 sixth-form students from across London with a series of skills workshops in a university environment, one-to-one mentoring at an architecture practice and in-depth guidance on university applications. At the end of the year, students' work is usually displayed in a public exhibition.

that model captured the bonding of my beloved Architectural Association unit, enjoying an autumn weekend in Bedford Square in 1988.

The light entering the room from the west dissected all these unrelated fragments, but at the same time united them all, reinforcing their connections. I could not think of a clearer visual metaphor for our year-one studio culture. In my office today, on the fifth floor at The Bartlett, I cherish a few models and photos that survived at least half a dozen packing and unpacking rituals. They embody so many memories and a deep feeling of longing for those years past.

What is a fragment?

FP: As we can see in the ever-growing collection of objects that have invaded our teaching studios and offices over the years, the term 'fragment' can denote two different ideas: one is of the dislocated object taken away from its original context and the other is of an object that is started but is incomplete, unfinished. So it can be a small piece that has come off a larger whole, a part of something else, a broken piece, a detached piece, a scrap, something unfinished, fractured, lost or less than a whole.

In this chapter, we focus on three fundamental qualities of the term fragment: *incomplete, broken* and *displaced*. What are the material and immaterial qualities, the magic embodied in these three notions? How do they become an inspiration, a catalyst that triggers imagination, and provide a sense of belonging in our architectural endeavours and teaching practice? Particularly relevant to us is how the displaced fragment relates to its original context; its absence creates numerous ways that the fragment alludes to and is deeply evocative of that origin. Displaced objects are embodied with a special power: that of memory. They relate to a time and a place, and are invaluable ingredients in cultivating experimentation when thinking about design. It is the personal associations, the memories of places, situations, and people that are embedded within these objects, which give them meaning and relevance. The ever-growing collections of models, relics and personal items are an invaluable teaching tool, a record of past achievements, and a key element of studio culture explored further in chapter four.

Collecting is personal and is driven by personality, but through these objects of the collection, the personal becomes shared, and so personality becomes physical. Collecting is often driven by chance, change and available opportunities; it depends on circumstance, the cultural context, and can be surprisingly revealing of our lives at particular times. Collecting can be planned, or a spontaneous and accidental activity, and is deeply dependant upon the places and spaces we wander through, inhabit, or choose to construct. Collecting fragments is also a way to bond with a place; to connect minds through discussion on symbolism and meaning; and to cultivate a sense of belonging with not only the immediate and present but also a more profound sense, which is rooted in our past and connects to the present, alluding to unknown future lives.

Collections are always changing and never complete. This open-endedness, the indeterminacy, unknown, and constant adjustment, are all invaluable qualities in architectural thinking and practice. Collections have a personality, they are part of our personal growth and are expressive of the collector's interests, eccentricities, mind, spirit and soul.

Packing and unpacking any collection of fragments can be exciting, traumatic, delicate, and exhausting. Walter Benjamin perhaps best describes the feeling this evokes in his essay 'Unpacking My Library: A Speech on Collecting'.[2] This catharsis of packing and unpacking, reorganising, opening up, and closing, is in parallel to reopening forgotten old lives, worlds and memories. It is a vital act in nurturing our identity. The juxtapositions and relationships between the various fragments, as well as the spaces in between them, are often as important as the pieces themselves; every time they are packed and unpacked these relationships dissolve, and new conversations start to evolve between them and the audience. A lot is physically and mentally eroded, but at the same time the connections between them form new readings and meanings.

JM: Fragments, whether objects or concepts of completeness and incompleteness, have been debated almost as long as any issue in Western architectural discourse, so it is not surprising that fragments are an important element in Pimenides' teaching practice. The controversy around Gothic's status as a unified whole or assembly of random parts, for example, is legendary, but the prevailing views of fragments took a decisive turn in the Renaissance.[3] During that period, the numerous remains of Roman

2. Walter Benjamin, 'Unpacking My Library', *Illuminations*, edited by Hannah Arendt, Schocken, 1969, pp. 69–82.
3. The perception of Gothic as 'barbaric' because it is incomplete, widely held during the Renaissance, is touched on in James Ackerman, '"ARS Sine Scientia Nihil EST" Gothic Theory of Architecture at the Cathedral of Milan', *The Art Bulletin*, vol. 31, no. 2, 1949, pp. 84–111. This deals with the completion of Milan Cathedral, started as a Gothic building but remaining incomplete well into the Renaissance era. One point of debate was whether it would be less offensive if finished as a Gothic edifice, for all the 'faults' of that style, or whether it would be better to try to adapt it to the 'coherence' of the Renaissance. Gothic's apparent capacity for changefulness and individual inventiveness is part of what appealed to John Ruskin, see John Ruskin, 'The Nature of Gothic', *The Stones of Venice*, vol. II, 1904, pp. 180–279; *The Library Edition of The Works of John Ruskin*, edited by Edward Tyas Cook and Alexander Wedderburn, vol. X, George Allen, 1903-12.

architecture, which had loomed large but long been ignored – in, for example, Rome, Milan, Verona, Split, Nimes and Aix-la-Chapelle – began to be objects of curiosity and study. Initially, these ruins were didactic instruments to enable contemporary architects to recreate the glories for ancient classical civilisation, but prevailing intellectual beliefs during the Renaissance were strongly in favour of unity, with incompleteness seen as grotesque and an affront to taste. So, during the Neo-classical period in the 18th century, there were numerous schemes for physical restoration, completion and copying.

Selecting historic fragments for their didactic use is healthy because it encourages a live dialogue with a dead culture, as opposed to mimicking historical reproductions. The user does not mimic but, instead, interprets all stories, qualities and ideas, with radically new pieces emerging from this dialectic engagement. These fragments can be visible or invisible, imagined or remembered, and all are connected to people and places.

Fragments as spurs to memory

FP: Our memories enable us to be who we are, they become alive and interact with us through the presence of various objects. It is the silent dialogue, the associations we develop with particular objects that is the starting point for inspiration and exploration. This is a fundamental design and teaching tool. Those relics with their potent memories and physical and invisible qualities are a type of library of life. They become animated, live ghosts, juxtaposed characters, creating parallel lives for reference and inspiration.

Remembering is selective, and the more we cultivate our memory in diverse fields, the more we are able to make connections between incompatible worlds. This is a very effective way to improve our creativity and imagination. Remembering and imagining are deeply interconnected and by definition are fragmentary operations, always unfinished and incomplete; it is this incompleteness or fragmentation that the student or architect should be inspired by and which they should regard as an opportunity and framework for possible solutions.

JM: We have seen that fragments can become physical analogues of memories. Their specific material qualities and their physical presence trigger memories of situations, places, territories, and people. They enable a powerful interaction between the visible and the invisible.

Fragments also connect the personal experiences to a wider cultural context, the context of their origin, which can be interpreted differently by everyone. The power of a physical paper photograph capturing a moment can become an anchor of memories between people, enabling us to make connections and speculate about unknown missing parts, and extend into imaginary and unknown fields. Memory is the great foundation for imagination; it restores identity and personal meaning, and this latent memory comes from within the objects.

Memory, the impressions it evokes and the creative opportunities they invite, is central to the role of fragments in teaching. Memory is not, however, entirely a random phenomenon. It can be structured and organised, both to make it more effective in and for an individual, but also to show how it might connect to collective memory and so to culture itself. We shall explore several means for doing this, which have some relevance to Pimenides' teaching practice. These include the Renaissance concept of the memory theatre, as explained by Frances Yates.[4] This concept supports Pimenides' belief that that memory is visual and spatial, with connections made between individual memories and associated images, places, people and objects.

Another important intellectual device that connects memory and culture, via images, is an idea developed by the art historian Aby Warburg, who came from a famous Hamburg banking family and founded the Warburg Institute, which moved to London in the 1930s. He devoted much of the last years of his life to developing the concept he called Mnemosyne, which proposes that a relatively small number of archetypal images, not original paintings or sculptures, could be assembled into a relationship with each other where, for their own and collective qualities, they could evoke different aspects of a conception of culture.[5] The ideas they contain and the memories they awaken, which are necessarily subjective, could coalesce in individuals' consciousness into compatible but not necessarily identical notions of culture. Pimenides' own collection of images recalls Warburg's *Mnemosyne Atlas* in a powerful but allusive, and elusive, way. We shall explore this later in the chapter. First though, Pimenides expands on the role of fragments in her teaching practice.

4. See Frances Yates, *The Art of Memory*, University of Chicago Press, 1966. This book helped to inaugurate research into the relationship between memory, images, and space. Yates, a doyenne of The Warburg Institute, drew on its founder Aby Warburg's work on images, iconography and appreciation of Renaissance, European and Classical culture.
5. See Ernst Gombrich, *Aby Warburg: An Intellectual Biography*, University of Chicago Press, 1970. According to Gombrich, this 'vast pictorial symphony' took 'the form of a "picture atlas", the title of which would be Mnemosyne', p. 283.

3.2

3.3

FP: Remembering fractions of our past reminds us of the journeys we have taken, what we learned and people we met, and eventually it becomes a form of slowly but steadily discovering, deeper and more clearly, who we are. It helps us restructure our values and shapes our future. This would be impossible without the presence of these relics; these amazing sources of hope and life that, when moved and reorganised, can cause an earthquake of memory. It is something like magic: the connections that we are able to achieve are only possible due to the human capacity to remember.

Most of the time these memories are fragmented rather than coherent, so remembering is like dreaming, always a fluid alchemy of continuous or fragmented experiences. I sometimes feel that without physical relics of these past worlds, my memory and capacity to imagine and create will dissolve. I need these physical visual references to remind me who I am, what influenced me in my formative years back in Athens and while studying and working here in London and further afield.

Fragments and collecting

FP: In the year-one studio, our collections and archived objects were accommodated in offices, corridors, ceilings, storerooms, bins, and skips. This has been an archive of objects that is not only a tool for demonstrating design ideas and skills, but also something more special: the parallel lives of the original creator, the tutor analysing it and the student interpreting it in various possible options. These archived fragments, by definition, connect us to the past but are also the basis for future visions and imaginative readings.

The fragility of most of these objects makes it impossible to efficiently pack and move them. The way they are collected, displayed and juxtaposed on the shelves and in cabinets depends upon personal cataloguing systems. By displacing these objects in order to pack, one erodes memories and destroys connections between them, yet is filled with optimism, as they are all items of immense value. Unpacking all types of models, one realises, is a great lesson in logical and structural thinking, as gravity and insulation are two key elements critical to their survival. Well-packed objects seem settled covered in bubble wrap, foam or newspaper, sleeping peacefully for months in crates. These were twice packed and unpacked, first for temporary accommodation and then, after three years, returned and reinstalled in their final home, the refurbished 22 Gordon Street. About 30 per cent of the contents broke, were stolen or not robust enough to survive, emotionally or physically, the forces of three moves.

The importance of fragments in design education

FP: Fragments enable the individual to connect to a discussion, through impression, as well as memory. They allow us to have a choice of interacting with them and find relevant meaning, allowing for more dialogue, freedom in discovering one's own interests, and relevant territories to get involved with. It is through the relics I have collected over the years that the lives of these objects can be reconstituted, re-enter our present and become a stronger network. It is vital to cultivate an ability to critically connect irrelevant and unrelated pieces, to develop an open mind and receptive eye to see things afresh.

Fragments have a close relationship to memory. Memory is by definition a fragmentary operation, though imagining and remembering are interconnected, always unfinished and incomplete. The quality of incompleteness can serve as inspiration for the architect. While qualities of incompleteness and fragmentation could be perceived as a weakness, they can also be seen as an opportunity, scaffolding, or framework for possible solutions.

Fragments are always part of their context, sometimes well known, at others entirely unknown and mysterious, eroded physically or in our memories. The idea that a piece, a fragment of something, can represent the whole, the essence of a context, is vital in architectural thinking and various traditions of representation. For example, Le Corbusier's diagrammatic sketches of the Acropolis setting or Dimitri Pikionis' stone paving of the Panathenaic route, discussed in chapter two, are very poignant examples: the first is representing the place, the second is constructing it. It is the absence of their context that is so powerful and allows for a myriad of associations to inspire us.

Forming the core of my thinking when I was asked back in the 1990s to write the curriculum for the year-one design course was that in order to cultivate creativity in students designing their first building, we should give them a series of preliminary projects of various scales, that oscillate between systematic analysis and more fresh and intuitive responses to various situations. An example was how a feast can help a young architecture student to understand human behaviour and the richness, complexity and possibilities of a collective culture. Architecture is not only designing walls; more difficult to understand is why you need a wall in the first place and how the character of a wall can help a specific situation. Then we can go on designing it.

Architectural design is a peculiar constant dialogue between logical decisions and all sorts of personal inspirations, memories, and experiences. The dialogues between unrelated fragments from different worlds, unplanned alchemies that are invaluable inspiration for imagining new worlds, only start to exist in our minds. We need to understand the power of these fragments, whether as an idea or object, as catalysts, as powerful tools enabling us as architects, teachers and students to wonder, wander and dream of unknown worlds, and to construct in our minds then translate into reality.

Collecting objects enables and inspires students to cultivate their improvisation and adaptability. It gives us teachers the opportunity to teach hands-on crafting skills and to explore what students are trying to communicate and to encourage the investigation of connections between unrelated ideas; all fundamental skills that an architect has to learn. From the point of view of a collection, any object within it is a fragment of the whole.

The images in this chapter show some of the typical amassed collections of models found in my office. I use these models, many of which are fragments, to discuss and illustrate the possibilities for students' designs. For example, one might talk about how the embryonic form of *this* little plaster cast later turned into *this* design sketch, which then developed into *this* building... so, having already made one cast yourself, how could you proliferate your initial ideas in a similar way to develop that design?

The fact that these fragments are diverse and irrelevant to each other helps keep the students' interpretations free, reflecting their interests and personalities. I might emphasise to them that these teaching tools are not to be copied, but are potential catalysts, stepping-stones in design inspiration and processes of making. For me, the relationships between the various piled-up pieces are a big part of the inspiration, and so, incomplete models, as well as perfectly crafted ones, become starting points of thinking for the students. For a first-year student, it is vital to cultivate the ability to critically connect irrelevant and often unrelated pieces, develop design imagination and see unknown possibilities. Collecting, referring, remembering, studying, reconfiguring and producing multiple parallel readings of these fragments becomes a healthy starting point for design exploration.

Is collecting a disease, a tool, or just a pleasure? At the very least, objects have mnemonic qualities, evoking, for instance, the first sight of them or the moment of their acquisition. If the collecting urge is structured, that structure becomes an element of memories too. So, building a collection of fragments can help the imagination to run across time, possibly even whole epochs. This can transport students into new and unfamiliar imaginative space, such as remembering the past and imagining the future as a seamless intellectual and creative exercise. This is critical to my teaching practice and was the inspiration behind the title of this book. Memory, in this scenario, becomes a tool for imagining new possible realities. This reconfiguration and multiple parallel readings and lives of these fragments become a very healthy starting point for design explorations. The interpretation comes from three parts: the creator, the archivist and the student. From these spring all possible interpretations. Once these examples are available to a student, then all sorts of stories can be built upon that help to develop an attitude or philosophy towards design ideas and methods.

Another aspect that is interesting is how time dilutes the physical materiality, qualities and stories related to these collections, making them a perfect register of time. Some of them were initially two dimensional, but with ageing are transformed into three-dimensional items, which reveal a number of beautiful geometrical surprises. The colour fading, dust accumulation, material dislocation and shifts, all tell stories about these objects' lives. The transformation and distortion of the original object is inspiration for new readings by students. These pieces and relics are especially powerful in how they interconnect through different authors' personalities. Every student that revisits someone else's pieces makes totally different connections and imagines possible adjustments.

Collecting is an opportunity to teach students how to improvise, sharpen their mind, judgment, personality and imagination. Developing a skill of making connections is one of the fundamental qualities an architect has to learn, as it expands their ability to collaborate, care, and have readiness. It is the critical and creative mind, looking at the world afresh, that making connections helps with.

Through our collaboration with the Sir John Soane's Museum, over eight years, which we describe in chapter five, other worlds opened up, and new notions of what a fragment might be entered our educational debates. Pieces from the Soane's collection broadened our horizon and definitions of fragment, and inspired our ever-growing collections in our own studios. In a nutshell, every year a series of objects from the Soane's collection was given to us as the starting point for our six-week installation project. These objects were, in a way, the clients for which our constructed installation pieces were designed and built. Initially, we studied each object, understood its historical and material qualities, ideas and purpose. Then students, individually and

3.4

3.5

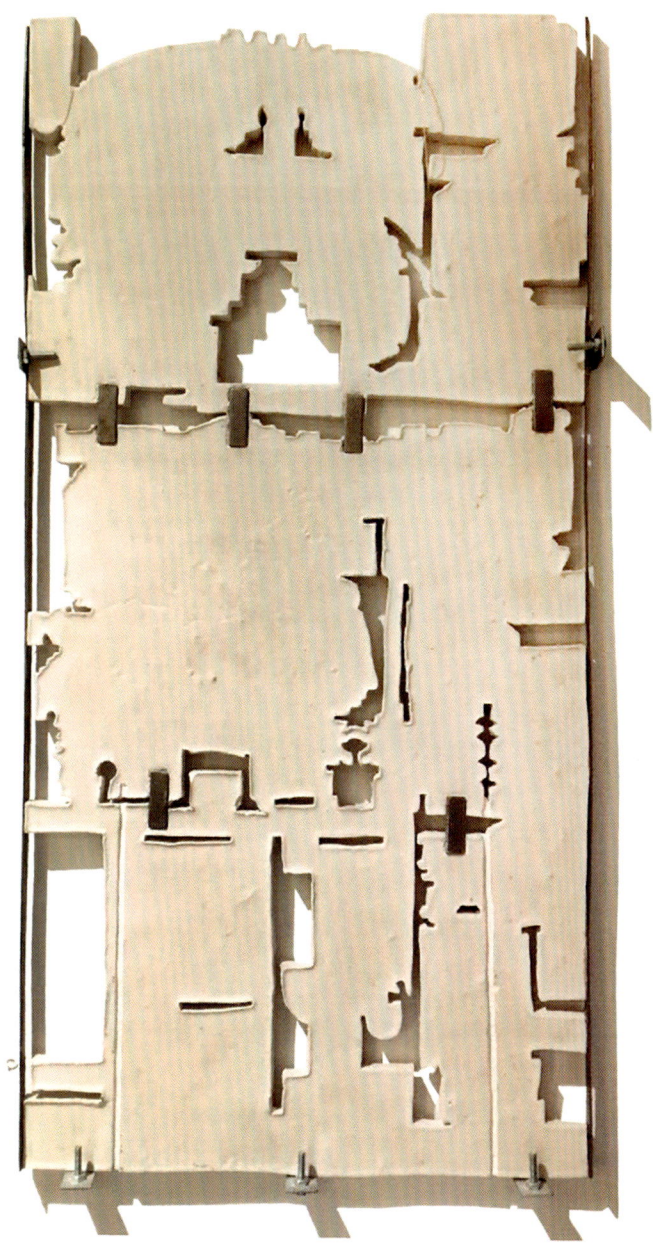

3.6

collectively, interpreted these objects, abstracted their readings, and started brainstorming how completely new designs would capture the essence of all this. Ultimately, these newly fabricated structures by year-one students would temporarily be installed in Pitzhanger Manor's spaces, adjusting their function and character.

Sir John Soane's Museum in Lincoln's Inn Fields is the ultimate kingdom of collecting fragments from the world. These, together with other themes and stories, became the core of year-one installation projects for eight years. Specific fragments from the Soane's collection were interpreted and informed a series of new, larger, spatial fragments, designed and constructed as a means of adjusting given locations. With all the associations and possible readings by groups of year-one students, these objects were the inspiration for new occupations of historic places. Working with Sir John Soane's Museum helped us to refine and stretch the limits of students' concepts of the notion of the fragment.

From our 2018 Hackney Wick canal installation, it was not only the six site-specific designs that stayed in our memories. What was memorable about the occasion was the spirit of a spontaneous multi-layered orchestration on a dark and chilly winter evening: the reflected light fragments on the canal; the sound of dripping water upon metallic sheets; the scrumptious taste of baked delicacies and mulled wine; the voices of alumni, critics, and happy and tired students resting on benches, surprised by the idea that celebration is a vital aspect of an architect's life; Venetian 18th-century music mixed with improvised Ottoman-inspired compositions; the floating fragments of faces; model icebergs the students had constructed; and lights scattered in the night over the canal. There were also pieces of text by Ruskin and our former director of The Bartlett School of Architecture Philip Tabor, at present a resident of Venice. It was a multiplicity of various happenings, with people participating, exchanging jokes, music and critiques; a proper event at an interestingly problematic London place. Students and guests experienced how architecture is all about life and people, which is what made that evening so memorable and rewarding. It is an example of how a collection of fragments communicates the spirit and ideas of the whole – building, event and momentary experience – more than a complete assembly of its parts. It remains in the mind as a series of fragments.

For our annual field trip in 2018, we visited Venice during a weekend of dramatic floods. The picture of a church façade reflected in a puddle (p. 124) tells a wonderful story about that specific day in late November, when the flooding in the Veneto area was alarming. I love that this picture talks in a very poetic, clear and precise way about the planet sinking. That puddle of canal water represents a fragment of an imaginary island of water, lying on the ground in Venice. With the planet being abused more and more, this upside-down picture says it all, and who is to say what is real or unreal, reflected or actual?

Architectural design is a constant and peculiar dialogue of rational and logical decisions and facts, together with an array of personal inspirations, associations, past and imaginary moments, experiences, and dreams. These latter elements derive and are born from the soul, mind, instinct, empathy, stomach, and often by accident. It is this constant dialogue of various fragments from all these worlds, experiences and lives, that gives us the spine, ammunition, strength and inspiration to imagine new worlds, spatial qualities, possibilities, and structures; whether rationally, consciously, or by instinct.

These fragments are vital in the design process. A piece of orchestral music is dead unless it is performed. It needs the various instruments, as well as the connecting and bonding soul, which is the conductor. Each time and place the piece is performed, it is always different. Because of the specific alchemy of the performance, infinite variations occur. This is a very useful metaphor for how we can initiate a young, fresh student into the process of design, and the magic of never-ending decision-making. Louis Kahn indicated the fruitful relationship between intuition and memory when he wrote:

I was brought up when the sunlight was yellow, and the shadow was blue. But I see it clearly as being white light and black shadow. Yet this is nothing alarming, because I believe that there will come a fresh yellow, and a beautiful blue, and that the revolution will bring forth a new sense of wonder. Only from wonder can come our new institutions ... they certainly cannot come from analysis.[6]

I believe that the more we understand the power of fragments as a tool for wondering, simultaneously exposing one's mind to various unrelated pieces as a trigger for inspiration, the more we can help and guide fresh minds to imagine and be inventive.

In 2016, we returned to The Bartlett's original home at 22 Gordon Street. Over the last 25 years, first-year students have created about 2,000 models in a process that is instrumental for initiating architectural thinking, exploring spatial qualities and expressing personalities. This invaluable

6. Louis Kahn, *Conversations with Students*, Princeton Architectural Press, 2000, pp. 14–5.

archive of models has served two purposes: a reference for skills, ideas, range of materials and scales, and a springboard for initiating new readings and interpretations. Part of this archive is made out of intact objects, such as models in scales ranging from 1:1000 to 1:20, and 1:1 prototypes, and the other is made out of fragmented, incomplete test pieces – dusty and scruffy, weathered materials that serve as a memory of the past and as design inspiration for the future. Time, use and memory hold a lot of secrets and past stories that the original authors possess or understand. These models also allow for new interpretations and multiple readings for someone who has never seen them before. The point of this first exercise is to discover, or rather to invent, the secrets of these models between the dust and the memories they carry. Students, within tutorial groups, collectively choose an individual model and are then asked to dig, select, and excavate the most intriguing aspects, qualities and ideas.

In order to appreciate the importance of fragments in our teaching world and tradition, it is useful to refer to a typical brief for the first project of the year, which explains the multiple connections between found and constructed fragments. In September 2016, this project had three purposes:

1. To introduce the basic culture and representation of architecture by learning how to record those strange objects as if they are archaeological finds.
2. To cultivate a culture of looking critically at things and the world. Assume nothing, question a lot and be curious. Learn to express your own personality and mind in whatever you study.
3. To explore given fragments that come from a collection, which you share no memory of, and by personally interpreting them gradually become more and more connected to them, slowly entering the past world and the family of the school, building up a personal story to communicate memories and future dreams.

The students were encouraged to use a range of representational techniques, which explore the following questions: How do you see this artefact as an unrelated, displaced fragment? What are the ideas and qualities of the artefact that you are interested in recording and communicating? How can you bring your own references, background, and experiences to handling and analysing this artefact?

Mnemonic fragments

JM: One of the purposes for which Pimenides uses fragments is to stimulate memory, often as a way of drawing out students' individual experience and to allow them to discuss it. In this way a fragment can become a form of 'objectification' of a subjective experience, allowing it to be shared. In a group, some students may share similar memories stimulated by the same object, while others may remember something quite different. This can lead to educationally stimulating discussions,[7] but there is a deeper level to this. Even though incomplete by definition – perhaps because of its incompleteness – the fragment invites an imaginative attempt to recreate and so to appreciate its context and origins. A fragment is not just a route to draw out a student's personal memories; it also offers a pathway to relate their own experiences to a wider cultural condition.

The relationship between fragments, memories and wider cultural systems have attracted the attention of scholars for millennia. This brings us back to Aby Warburg and his Mnemosyne project. Warburg's thought is notoriously subtle and hard to categorise, so the following remarks are hardly definitive, and draw heavily on the account given by Warburg's follower, Ernst Gombrich.[8] In essence, the Mnemosyne project is an attempt to evoke a broad conception of the culture of the Renaissance – the focus of Warburg's efforts as a scholar – through a series of carefully selected images. For these purposes, he did not want to use original paintings or pieces of sculpture, but reproductions of them. Their fame made them immediately recognisable, at least to anyone who Warburg considered 'cultured'. They can be assembled into a relationship with each other where, for their own and collective qualities, they evoke different aspects of culture. The ideas they contain, which Warburg defined with some objective precision, as evidenced by his work on iconography, and the memories they awaken, that necessarily reside

---

7. It is important for this purpose that the object is a fragment, as it invites imagination to 'complete' it, i.e. to imagine it as a whole or part of a whole. Should the object appear to be complete in and of itself, it is unlikely to stimulate such discussion, as students will recognise it or, worse, attempt to 'second guess' why they have been shown it. In either case the object ceases to be a route into the students' personal experience, and becomes more akin to a piece of received knowledge. The phenomenon of 'incompleteness', or at least an obligation on the viewer/observer to complete a work is important in certain types of modern and contemporary art. It was identified by Umberto Eco in *The Open Work*, Harvard University Press, 1962. Eco wrote, '"Informal art" is open in that it proposes a wider range of interpretive possibilities, a configuration of stimuli whose substantial indeterminacy allows for a number of possible readings, a "constellation" of elements that lend themselves to all sorts of reciprocal relationships.' (p. 84) He continues, 'Sculpture shows us yet another way of approaching the open work: the plastic forms of Gabo or Lippold invite the viewer to participate actively in the polyhedral nature of the works.' (p. 85) Eco sees the origin of this in the idea of movement depicted in paintings, an obvious fiction which demands that viewers make an imaginative leap, and so begin to 'complete' the work for themselves. '... the viewer can (indeed, must) choose his own points of view, his own connections, his own directions...' (p. 86). The point here is that , again, we find in Pimenides' teaching practice echoes of sophisticated contemporary aesthetic and cultural thinking.
8. Gombrich, *Aby Warburg*, 1970. See Chapter XV, 'The Last Project: MNEMOSYNE', pp. 283–306.

in the subjective, coalesce in individual consciousness into notions of culture which are compatible with but not necessarily identical to those of other individuals. As some of the best known and most familiar works of art, Warburg's images were in many cases complete in and of themselves. The intellectual context in which he placed them, however, made them fragments of a greater whole – in short, Renaissance culture – into which they offered a series of partial portals.

There are of course many differences between Mnemosyne and Pimenides' teaching practice. One of the most important is that for Warburg the system underlying Mnemosyne is largely objective as it exists outside of individual consciousness and independently of the images themselves – if never wholly knowable at least by a single individual – but for Pimenides the whole is largely a subjective creation, though with the external support of guidance from tutors and other influences.[9] It can only come into effect through personal effort from an individual as a form of synthesis. External influences, though, lend a degree of objectivity, or at least quasi-objectification, that allows the individual's efforts to be shared, if only in part, and so discussed.

Why, then, is Warburg even remotely relevant to understanding Pimenides' ideas? While repeating the provisos mentioned above, that Warburg's thought is notoriously complex and allusive so it is hard to answer this question specifically, several points might tentatively be proposed. As Gombrich writes, Mnemosyne was formed around 'two main strands... the vicissitudes of the Olympian gods in the astrological tradition and the role of the ancient pathos formulae in post-mediaeval art and civilisation',[10] both of which find echoes in Pimenides' thinking. Other affinities include: Pimenides' appreciation of images, both as records of certain visual phenomena in themselves, which might on occasion be termed 'memories', and as fragments of a larger whole, from which that whole might be partially reconstructed; and, to extrapolate from that point, her belief that some concept of principles and ideas underlie these visible phenomena, whose understanding and sharing might benefit creative thought. The dynamic between image, memory and the way they can be shared might tentatively be proposed as one possible introduction to the concept of culture.

<hr />

9. Warburg, argues Gombrich, in a chapter suggestively named 'The Theory of Social Memory', drew on certain ideas current in the early 20th century, which proposed that memory achieved a certain degree of 'objectivity', or at least collectivity, and so became embedded in collective consciousness, rather than purely subjective concepts: '... the artist who comes into touch with these symbols once more experiences the "mnemic [i.e. based on collective, culture memory] energies" with which they were charged'. Gombrich, *Aby Warburg*, 1970, p. 244.
10. Gombrich, *Aby Warburg*, 1970, p. 283.

In the early stages of working on this book, Pimenides' use of images – often quickly taken photographs printed at fairly low resolutions, which prevented them being seen as 'finished' or 'perfected' – impressed itself on me as we talked. To try to test or exorcise this sensation, I took a series of her images and tried to arrange them as a grid where one axis represented different locations and the other ideas, placing each where I felt it fitted best. At the very least, this exercise provided a way for me to enter into Pimenides' mental world, and after an initial surprise at seeing the grid she agreed, and it became the basis for subsequent discussion about the relationship between image, memory and fragment, even as its importance and illegitimate and tenuous descent from Warburg faded into insignificance.

While there is some affinity between the Mnemosyne project and Pimenides' notion of image, fragment and memory – as the former takes images, though possibly complete and certainly complex in themselves, as representative fragments through which a greater whole can be appreciated – this should not be pushed too far.

More significant for understanding Pimenides' teaching practice are radical changes in the role of fragments in architectural discourse during the early 19th century, themselves indicative of important intellectual developments of the time. A brief exploration of these developments might help to indicate how her appreciation of fragments takes us to the heart of Western cultural discourse.

These developments include Giambattista Vico's concept of metonymy, as interpreted by Isaiah Berlin, and by the architect and educator Richard Patterson in elucidating Emil Kaufman's essay 'Three Revolutionary Architects: Boullée, Ledoux and Lequeu' (1952).[11] The concept of fragments is also the focus of architectural historian Robin Middleton's study of Sir John Soane, whose work, as we have seen, played an important role in the development of Pimenides' teaching practice.[12] According to Middleton, these changes had several roots. Some came from the picturesque movement, which found pleasure in the rawness of ruins for its own sake rather than a cautionary tale on the perils of incompleteness. Overall, the new

11. Isaiah Berlin, 'The Philosophical Ideas of Giambattista Vico', *Vico and Herder*, Chatto and Windus, 1978/80, pp. 1–142; Richard Patterson, 'Three Revolutionary Architects: Boullée, Ledoux, Lequeu', *Architecture and the Sites of History: Interpretations of Buildings and Cities*, edited by Iain Borden and David Dunster, Butterworth Architecture, 1995, pp. 149–62; and Emil Kaufman, 'Three Revolutionary Architects: Boullée, Ledoux, and Lequeu', in *Transactions of the American Philosophical Society*, vol. 42, no. 3, 1952, pp. 431–564. The most relevant text by Vico is Giambattista Vico, *The New Science*, 1725. *Architecture and the Sites of History* was a record of the 'contextual' course, run as an introduction to history and theory for Bartlett undergraduates during the 1980s. It was conceived and run by a group which included David Dunster and Adrian Forty. Many of the people mentioned in this book contributed to it, including, beyond those cited, the construction economist Graham Ive and Jeremy Melvin.
12. Robin Middleton, 'Soane's Spaces and the Matter of Fragmentation', *John Soane: Architect: Master of Space and Light*, edited by Margaret Richardson and MaryAnne Stevens, Royal Academy of Arts, 1999, pp. 26–37.

sensibility to and appreciation of fragments, according to Middleton, is one of the inaugural features of what was in the early 19th century emerging as a modern world view.[13] It also serves as the base for understanding how Pimenides uses the notion of fragments.

Middleton makes Soane an important figure in the intellectual shift on the attitude to fragments in the late 18th and early 19th centuries. We shall examine and develop Middleton's interpretation of the place of fragments and fragmentation in Soane's work, and from that outline their role in Pimenides' teaching practice. Along the way we will explore how her ideas relate to the significant place of the subject in broader architectural discourse, as in other chapters, showing how her teaching practice both relates to it and modifies in particular and important ways.

Middleton finds a particular sense of fragmentation in Soane's work. Drawing on an argument proposed by the art critic Jonathan Crary in his book *Techniques of the Observer* (1990), Middleton relates, in a very brief summary of his argument, how several developments at the beginning of the 19th century brought this new sense about and affected Soane's individual abilities and experience.[14] Among the new 'techniques' are a changing appreciation of colour, brought about by the painter JMW Turner – several of whose works Soane owned – and Goethe's *Theory of Colours*.[15] In Soane's hands this provoked a fragmentation of conventional concepts of space.

Middleton also adduces the influence of, among others, John Locke's concept of space in 'An Essay Concerning Human Understanding' (1689) and Lord Kames' more architecturally explicit analysis of the space of rooms.[16] From this privileging of sense over tradition and rationality as the bases for architecture came the picturesque, which expressly sought exquisite, piquant and subjective emotions in the experience of moving through space – in this case largely landscapes or gardens. All of these find the prime means for appreciating space in the senses and sensory experience.

---

13. Patterson, 'Three Revolutionary Architects', *Architecture and the Sites of History*, 1995, makes a similar point: 'In the work of the three architects we are about to look at... [Boullée, Ledoux and Lequeu]... we begin to see clear evidence that something new and very different was beginning to happen' (p. 150). He goes on to suggest that they challenged conventions of form and composition as part of a 'radically new vision of authority'. This vision was in turn based on a rejection of metaphor – favoured by their baroque predecessors – in favour of metonymy, which led, among other consequences to 'meaning' in architecture becoming dependent on representation of function.
14. Patterson, 'Three Revolutionary Architects', *Architecture and the Sites of History*, 1995, p. 26. Also Jonathan Crary, *Techniques of the Observer: On Vision and Modernity in the Nineteenth Century*, The MIT Press, 1990.
15. See Von Goethe, Johann Wolfgang, *Theory of Colours*, 1810, English translation by Charles Lock Eastlake, John Murray, 1840.
16. John Locke, *An Essay Concerning Human Understanding*, 1695, republished many times, e.g. Penguin Classics, 1997. Locke, as Middleton points out in 'Soane's Spaces and the Matter of Fragmentation', seeks to define all forms of knowledge including that of architectural space as deriving from sensory experience, which is the essence of what Locke contributes to a new understanding of space. Middleton draws attention to Locke's chapters on space, 'Of Space and Its Simple Modes' (pp. 99–108) and time, 'Of Duration' (pp. 108–19), as well as how they might combine, 'Of Extension and Duration considered together' (pp. 119–23). Middleton also refers to Lord Kames, *Elements of Criticism*, 1762.

Turning to Soane's experience and capabilities, Middleton finds him wanting as a conventional academic architect in terms of massing and composition. His ability, Middleton argues, lies in his skill at manipulating space in two ways: first, to slot and mould large, impressive spaces to predetermined, irregular boundaries, as at the Bank of England and the Law Courts, alongside Westminster Hall; second, to dematerialise the limits of space with abstract wall decoration, subtle colours and, above all, hidden light sources. In short, Soane was not just putting sensory experience at the fore, he was inviting the senses to be the guide to understanding the impressions his work gave, assembling these fragments, both literal and metaphorical, or impressionistic, into some element of 'objectified' coherence though subjective means. Where neo-classical reconstructions of ancient ruins depended on the external, semi-objective means of the classical tradition, Soane – following and extending the notion of subjective experience from Locke to the Picturesque movement – puts the obligation to make sense of fragments onto the viewer. This lies at the root of how Pimenides incorporates fragments into her teaching practice.

The façade of Soane's house in Lincoln's Inn Fields has generally attracted less analysis than the interiors. Yet it presents at least two notions of fragmentation, alongside many fragments. The first is its reference to the south front of Robert Adam's Kedleston Hall (1765), which itself draws deeply on the Arch of Constantine in Rome (c.315 CE). Adam – an architect who Soane knew as a young man and admired in old age[17] – made some adjustments to the Roman design but ensured that the model was recognisable, especially to the grand tourists of the period.

What Soane did is rather remarkable: he retained the tripartite horizontal division – inevitable, in a London terraced house of this type – and hinted at, rather than repeat, the columns that were an integral part of the Arch of Constantine and Kedleston Hall, using no more than vestigial capitals without even marking where the rest of the columns might be, despite the extensive but simple relief decoration on other parts of the façade. These capitals, it may be suggested, are metonyms of the columns and the classical tradition.[18] It is important that, in being metonymic, it is the visual impression of the parts that implies their meaning, i.e. their representation of complete columns. Using the starkest physical means, interpreted through a literary

---

17. In 1833 Soane bought about 9,000 of Adam's drawings from his estate for £200. Middleton, 'Soane's Spaces and the Matter of Fragmentation', *John Soane*, 1999, p. 32.
18. A metonym is a figure of speech where a part of an object stands for the whole; examples include 30 sails meaning 30 ships and 40 head of cattle meaning 40 cows. See footnote 24.

concept with which Soane was probably unfamiliar, though he absorbed it intuitively, he tied his house into the mainstream of European architecture, and touches on broader cultural discourses.

Something similar is true of the interior, though achieved by different means. Here, Soane combined personal comfort, for example his water closet, with some of the most complex, for their time, variable spatial effects. For Middleton, fragmentation is intrinsic to Soane's design practice.[19] As he suggests, it is barely possible to see a single one of Soane's rooms in its entirety, let alone to imagine the whole building from one of those spaces, as it is for instance in a neoclassical/beaux arts building, where certain commonly understood rules allow the initiated to know the whole from a part. On top of that, paintings add to allegorical and narrative effects, for example Hogarth's *A Rake's Progress* (1732-34),[20] while fragments and plaster casts, too numerous to take in on a single occasion, suggest ideas beyond the literal, just as hidden light sources suggest spaces beyond those immediately perceivable. Satire is also present in the dog's tomb in a basement yard in the house – inscribed with the words 'Alas Poor Fanny', alluding to Hamlet's 'Alas poor Yorick'[21] – and possibly even in the sarcophagus of Seti I, the most prized element in Soane's collection.[22] Here, the overall and overwhelming effect is of metaphor – essences alluded to rather than embodied in the literal physicality of the objects – and experiences, changing with movement through the building and during the course of a day, are more important than single items or spaces. These are among the phenomena in Soane's work that caught the attention of the year-one teaching team and held it for so long. Working with and in Soane's Museum and Pitzhanger Manor helped them to explore the concept of fragments and their didactic uses.

Metaphor to metonym

JM: The shift, identified by Middleton, in the early 19th century from concepts of wholeness to assemblies of fragments parallels another

19. Middleton, 'Soane's Spaces and the Matter of Fragmentation', *John Soane*, 1999, p. 30, Middleton observes that 'Soane's spaces cannot be apprehended as a whole'.
20. Soane purchased *The Rake's Progress* from William Beckford in 1802 for 570 guineas. Gillian Darley, *John Soane: An Accidental Romantic*, Yale University Press, 1999, p. 145. The subject of the sequence, of the decline and fall of an aristocratic wastrel despite marriage to an heiress, may have appealed to him given the poor relationship he had with his sons, whom he blamed for his wife's death (pp. 235–36). The relationship was, however, quite nuanced, as he grieved deeply over the death of his elder son (p. 267).
21. William Shakespeare, *Hamlet*, Act 5, Scene 1. The phrase 'Alas poor Yorick! I knew him. Horatio' which Hamlet utters when the gravedigger exhumes the clown Yorick's skull, is almost as well known and frequently cited as the opening words of Hamlet's soliloquy 'To be or not to be...', from the same play, Act 3, Scene 1.
22. The sarcophagus occupied pride of place in the museum Soane created in his house. He was fascinated by the translucent quality of its alabaster, which would glow if lights were placed inside, implying that its occupant, Pharoah Seti I, was coming back to life. Darley, *John Soane*, 1999, p. 275.

development associated with early modern thought. Richard Patterson sees an analogous shift from metaphor to metonym, outlined in the art historian Emil Kaufmann's essay 'Three Revolutionary Architects: Boullée, Ledoux and Lequeu' (1952), and traceable back to Giambattista Vico's *The New Science* (1725).[23] It was this shift, argues Patterson, that cleared the way from the illusion and allusion of Baroque to the formal certainties of neoclassicism, and, in the hands of Kaufman's trio of revolutionary architects, to an association of form with function that prefigures aspects of modernism a century later, restricting the possibility of other meanings or significance.

'Metaphor' and 'metonym' are both complicated concepts and come from difficult aspects of literary theory. The historian Hayden White gives a succinct but challenging account of these concepts and their context in his book *Metahistory* (1973).[24] Though his purpose is to explore how literary concepts underlie historical writing, the essence to which White distils them gives another angle to look at Soane and, especially, his house in Lincoln's Inn Fields. Using literary constructs to deal with images and objects also finds support in Giambattista Vico, or at least Isaiah Berlin's interpretation of him, where he cites Joseph le Maistre: *'la pensee et la parole sont un magnifique synonyme'* (thought and word are a magnificent synonym).[25]

Vico, Berlin goes on to adumbrate, believed that words originated as labels for objects, but expanded from that base via metaphor and metonym into richer and more ambiguous concepts. In a skeletal interpretation, White suggests that metaphor implies non-literal, allusory characteristics that can be evoked by a literal image or real phenomenon, while metonym cites a literal part (fragment) of something that can be taken to stand for its whole, for example 20 head of cattle, where 'head' is a metonym for the whole cow.[26] This offers a way of looking at Soane's house in Lincoln's Inn Fields: the

---

23. Patterson, 'Three Revolutionary Architects', *Architecture and the Sites of History*, 1995, p. 151.
24. Hayden White, *Metahistory: The Historical Imagination in Nineteenth-Century Europe*, Johns Hopkins University Press, 1973. White's analysis of metonymy is relevant for our purposes. 'Irony, Metonymy, and Synedoche are kinds of Metaphor' he explains, but differ from metaphor and each other in important ways (pp. 34–6). Where metaphor implies a connection between two phenomena which depends on literal and figurative readings, irony implies an 'implicit negation of what is explicitly affirmed [by such a juxtaposition or comparison]' (p. 34), while synecdoche assumes a similar essence shared by the two phenomena. Metonymy, on the other hand, treats two parts as equivalent and able to stand for each other (head, cow; sail, ship). 'In metonymy, then,' he concludes, 'one can simultaneously distinguish between two phenomena and reduce on to the status of a manifestation of the other', (p. 35). It is at least arguable that this is precisely what Soane did with his use of parts of columns to stand for whole columns on the façade of his house (and by extension, the façade as a metonym of Kedleston Hall, by an architect he admired, and of a seminal work of classical architecture, the Arch of Constantine). White's thinking is enormously rich but elusive, and it is not suggested here as a 'blueprint' for understanding Pimenides' concept of fragments. Rather, it is introduced to give some context to the wider concept of the fragment, in particular in relation to Soane and other architects of his generation.
25. Isaiah Berlin, 'The Philosophical Ideas of Giambattista Vico', *Vico and Herder*, 1978/80, fn p.42. Berlin suggests that de Maistre may have taken the insight directly from Vico, as he was 'one of the few readers [of Vico] in his day'.
26. Patterson, 'Three Revolutionary Architects', *Architecture and the Sites of History*, 1995, suggests that the books depicted in Boullée's Royal Library project (1765), on which colonnades rest, are a metonym for the library itself and a representation of its function, p. 153.

façade, with its capitals shorn of columns, depends on metonymy, which allows us to infer the presence of the column from only one part, while the interior operates through metaphor. Both, as outlined above, offer different notions of fragmentation.

The room, revisited and understood

JM: We can see how the fragments in Pimenides' room are both exemplary and a collection of examples of architectural thinking, as well as, of course, a record, archive, and library of her work. Let us now turn to Pimenides' relationship with fragments, as shown in the organisation of her offices at The Bartlett. The main impression she tries to create is one of wonder, and secondarily to create a labyrinthine version of a memory theatre in which students' imaginations can wander, which echoes the words used by UCL's first professor of architecture TL Donaldson in 1841, when he described architectural education of the time as akin to 'wandering in a labyrinth of experiments'.[27]

Each of Pimenides' rooms, in their various locations at The Bartlett, has been dominated by the presence of fragments. These can be overwhelming and confusing given that, for example, rammed together on one shelf may be a family photograph, a spoon, a small stone purloined from a temple, a dissected bell from a church in East London, a dried African vegetable and a model from a student project. Their monetary value is irrelevant and their precise origin often a distraction. What matters is their character as objects. Such is the visceral presence of sequences of this sort that they are impossible to ignore. If the first impression may be confusing, the second is to try to engage with them. Individually, the fragments may be utterly banal in themselves, but even two banal objects, if sufficiently different, might start to define some sort of conceptual space between them. That space also exists in a real dimension as the distance between the objects, but might, though an imaginative operation, start to take on unreal, surreal or metaphorical qualities too. This exercise of the imagination comes close to design, though it needs a project brief to achieve that status fully.

These objects acquire a cluster of associations, over multiple viewings and discussions with numerous students, in groups or with individuals, in different rooms and covering many years. These associations are not inherent

27. Thomas Leverton Donaldson, Inaugural Lecture as the first Professor of Architecture at UCL, 1842, cited in the frontispiece in Jeremy Melvin and Bob Sheil, editors, *The Bartlett 175*, Architectural Review, 2016.

in the objects, but rather in the subjective memories and impressions of their viewers. Through discussion, these subjectivities might begin to overlap, for instance students being told that a certain fragment comes from a particular temple whose site, origin and history can be understood, and may entice them to introduce an element of shared, objective information in their assessment of it. In this manner, the myriad of associations starts to become a tradition of thought, in the sense that repetition of an association may cause it to become attached to a certain object, and so passed on to other people. The number of possible permutations of impressions and associations is incalculable, but fixed, or at least very slowly changing, points start to emerge. So what might appear at first sight to be, and may have originated as, a random collection of objects actually helps to shape Pimenides' teaching practice overall.

Every so often the arrangement of the fragments changes. New items are added and old ones taken away. Each alteration provokes subtle ripples in their individual and collective significance and interpretation. Between them there is a malleable, fluid and contingent, but loose, system of association, memory and meaning. It is this amorphous and strange phenomenon that becomes a powerful teaching tool. Its protean character does not just mean that there is no right or wrong way to engage with it; it also offers multiple ways of becoming engaged, which is vital for first-year students in particular, who come with an enormous range of experience and knowledge. Once they are engaged, they have something in common that allows them to learn from each other, and to be taught together. Indeed, inviting a group of students to discuss a set of fragments can be an extremely effective way of enabling them to find out about each other and their interests.

These associations, provoked by objects, have an express didactic purpose on several levels. One, as described above, is to provide diverse students with some common experience. This in turn relates to another aspect of Pimenides' teaching practice, studio culture, the subject of the next chapter. Her concept of fragments shares the notion of, and manifests, a culture forged from the interaction between information and inspiration. Students can of course engage positively with studio culture, but they can also experience it passively. To get the best out of fragments, they have to engage consciously and actively, and in doing so may challenge some of their existing ways of thinking and certainly extend them.

Similarly, the concept of fragments bears some relation to the way people and places play a part in Pimenides' teaching practice, as discussed in chapters one and two. The interactions between all of them are obviously

categorically and materially different, but underlying them is a range of possible ways of engaging with the subject of architecture. There is no predetermined entry point, rather a spectrum of options, which is fluid enough for one experience to start in one mode and switch into another. A student may start by deriving an idea from a fragment, which could then develop via a conversation with a tutor or in a piece of writing into a relationship with a particular place.

Each of these concepts provides some means for students to engage with a body of ideas, to navigate their own way through it and ultimately assemble their own conceptual cabinet of curiosities. Some ideas or pieces of information may bear strong similarities in more than one mode. Where they differ quantifiably is in their balance between subjectivity and objectivity, agency and passivity, individuality and collectivity, though in no case does one of these pairs completely occlude the other. Instead, they complement each other, cumulatively building students' experience in a structured but non-prescriptive way.

Pimenides' teaching practice permeates the idea that students have latent talents and perceptions connected to their prior experience. It is, therefore, important to discover who students are, where they come from, their identity and beyond that their being, mind, soul, character and personality, all strongly connected to their roots. Remembering is the base for imagining.

For Pimenides, fragments are more powerful than a whole. She rejects Robert Venturi's famous characterisation of fragments having an 'obligation toward the difficult whole'.[28] The whole is complete: a closed system of reduced poetic or imaginative possibility, especially where change or invention may be involved. The relationship between fragments and an often illusory whole can, however, still be important: they can be something broken off, or incomplete, and each condition has some purpose. A fragment might also be thought of as a small component of a different world, such as a complete pot being a fragment of a kitchen. In each or any of these ways they become clues for students to follow.

The 'status' of these objects has something in common with the role of words in Vico's thought, at least as understood by Berlin: a word may originally be allocated to a particular object or meaning, but these can gradually acquire further associations and implications, which then become

---

28. This is the title of chapter 10 of Robert Venturi, *Complexity and Contradiction in Architecture*, Museum of Modern Art, 1966, pp. 89–103.

modified in subsequent interpretations. One example of this expansion of possible meanings is the word 'Jove', first standing for 'sky' then evolving into the name for the father of the Olympian gods, and finally the source of thunder, terror and duty.[29] For the purposes of this chapter, the relevant point is the capability of a word to carry layers of meaning, connected by literal, metaphorical and allegorical levels. The sky is a real, if complicated and misunderstood, phenomenon: it appears to be the source of thunder, which implies the power and rage of Jove/Zeus. It is, for a non- or pre-scientific intelligence, perfectly logical.[30] Again borrowing Berlin's citation of Joseph le Maistre's comment that words and pictures are synonyms, helps to understand a particular but important subset of Pimenides' fragments: her photographs.

The photographs cover all sorts of subjects, including recording work, pages, notes, particular places and people. For the most part, they are taken to capture an immediate effect, not as finished, polished images, but they have all sorts of allusive qualities. Some are specifically identifiable such as Sydney Opera House; others intended to portray something more allusive, such as a spontaneous performance in a public place. They beg to be placed in some form of association, so that, as with the three-dimensional fragments, they begin to qualify and alter each other, to assemble into chains of association, dissolving into another almost as soon as one tries to fix them.

As well as a didactic tool, Pimenides' collections of fragments are a record of her teaching career. Some represent ideas she encountered long before she started teaching (for example, pictures of her family), others are objects found along the way, and still more are records or products of student work. Above all, though, the fragments imply incompleteness and so invite participants to complete them themselves. This exercise in completion, aided by ideas introduced in the educational process, encourages students to develop their own ideas, not just at an individual level, but also to enhance and develop their own systems of ideas or frames of reference.

FP: Concluding this chapter, I cannot think of a better example than to describe in brief the design and making process that took place during our

---

29. Berlin, 'The Philosophical Ideas of Giambattista Vico', *Vico and Herder*, 1978/80, p. 44.
30. On this specific point, consider Tolstoy's famous discussion of what might cause a train to move in the context of exploring the concept of causation. He proposes three possible explanations: the movement of the wheels, the apparently backward motion of the smoke, and the devil. Of these, the only 'complete' explanation is the devil, which for those who believe in such entities – in Tolstoy's formulation, a 'peasant' – is perfectly adequate and sufficient. The most 'accurate' explanation, the movement of the wheels, merely begs further questions such as what causes the wheels to move and so a chain of thinking that approximates to scientific enquiry. Leo Tolstoy, *War and Peace*, epilogue, part 2, chapter 3, translated by Rosemary Edmonds, Penguin, 1977, pp. 1408–9.

six magical years of collaboration with Sir John Soane's Museum, as represented in a group of 10-millimetre-thick plaster cast slices. Each of these is a simple cross-section through the museum itself. In a triumph of plaster casting technique, this very slender, ethereal body, held only by a steel ribbon, reverses what is solid and void in the real museum: the walls in section are translated as air and the atmosphere as a solid mass of plaster. This reversal alludes to the dense and rich memories of all the lives of the Soane family and 18th-century London society. The materiality of the slice is obedient to the rules of his collections, of which most were cast or stone. These five cast slices were installed in the old basement kitchen of Pitzhanger Manor. They referred to the kitchen's previous role as a cellar that served as a storage space for a number of Soane's casts. The ultimate transformation of these slices took place over a period of three hours on a cold December evening in 2008, when a series of floodlights projected their gigantic shadows upon the dusty walls of the basement. For a short period of time that evening, we danced and sipped mulled wine, surrounded by guests, shadows, and ghosts from centuries past.

3.8

3.9

3.10

3.11

3.12

Chapter 3 images

Photographs courtesy of Frosso Pimenides unless otherwise stated.

3.1 Pimenides' office (detail) in Wates House, May 2014. Photo: Robert Newcombe.

3.2 Pimenides' office (detail) in Wates House, June 2014. Photo: Robert Newcombe.

3.3 Pimenides' office (detail) in 22 Gordon Street, June 2019. Photo: Robert Newcombe.

3.4 A corridor teaching corner, surrounded by old student models. An installation project is suspended from the ceiling, taking the form of Soane's breakfast chair, as interpreted, designed, and constructed by students for Pitzhanger Manor, Ealing, London.

3.5 Timber and plaster columns from Pimenides' collection adorn the north corridor walls on the third floor at Wates House.

3.6 Plaster-cast reverse section – part of a series of slices – of Sir John Soane's Museum made by year-one students for the 2008 installation project. The plaster represents the real space filled with plaster casts in the museum; the gaps in the model indicate the position of solid walls and floors.

3.7 A fragment of a church façade is reflected in a puddle in Venice, after a dramatic rise in the water level, November 2018.

3.8 Pimenides' office in Wates House. Fragments of past installation pieces occupy the main working table, June 2014. Photo: Robert Newcombe.

3.9 'I would like to thank all the teas, coffees and lemonades that helped me write this book, and to all the people who picked the tea leaves and coffee beans and lemons from the trees, and to those people who made the beverages for me. Without them, this book would absolutely and certainly not exist'. Pimenides' office in Wates House, May 2014. Photo: Robert Newcombe.

3.10 & 3.11 Pimenides' office in Wates House, filled with fragments of installation pieces, models, and casts.

3.12 Pimenides' office at 22 Gordon Street, 2019.

Chapter 4:
Studio Culture

FROSSO PIMENIDES: There are many layers to educating a student in architecture: through lectures and public events; one-to-one and group tutorials; making in workshops; and design presentations, or 'crits' as we call them.[1] This raises fundamental questions about how architecture can be taught. Whatever the differences between various approaches, there is one common factor: the studio. It is the central space in students' learning lives, yet it seems to me that half of an individual's work ought to be pursued in privacy, while the other half is more collaborative. We will talk about the merits and features of both sides in some depth later on, but what seems vital to me is that students have access to a studio where both are possible. This chapter explores the importance of the studio as a set of spaces, which are always important to architects, and the working and collaborative culture that can emerge, with the right guidance, within them.

In the old style of doing things, a 'drawing office' was a place where architecture students had their big drawing boards and they would go to school to do that side of their work but perhaps not much else. Today, the studio is where nearly all teaching and communal or individual exchange is happening. It is a place where students have their own space, but is also where their tutorials take place; our studio has people working creatively, at the same time as others are being taught close by. So, students can create individually but also have the opportunity to listen to other tutorials that are going on. Aside from the more formal delivery of education, there is also something else going on that is like a group of musicians jamming in their living room.

In the first year, the majority of students have either come straight from school or have finished fairly recently. Most have been educated in a system focused, on the whole, on ticking boxes. Then they come to university in a

---

1 'Crits' (critiques) are presentations by students of their projects – at the end of a project and sometimes at interim points too – to a panel of tutors and external guests.

big, anonymous city, which is a challenge in its own right. It therefore seems important to create a special atmosphere, one where the first year is a stepping stone, providing them with a sense of belonging to a community before they move to the next phase of their education.

The physical studio has to give students the structure of the table, the chair, and the drawing board. It is a place to experiment, as well as where they put their tools, but it is also a place where they can look at and listen to each other, learn from each other and understand the value of different points of view. They might think: 'you can do better balsa models, I can do better plaster, we will learn from each other.' This is a valuable addition to what the more formal aspects of teaching can offer. The studio's main role, however, is to create a 'community of practice', where the students feel they share common values and beliefs, an environment of belonging, a common culture of trust. This then provides a common ground where they feel safe and confident to experiment, explore and make mistakes; a community where students feel they are not judged or that they have to produce successful results all the time, and where they can always rely upon each other for help. It is a place of generosity. Through working and socialising together in the studio, students develop trust and loyalty, and forge friendships that last a lifetime. Tutors, alumni and visitors come in and out, bringing with them inspiring ideas and objects they have encountered outside. In this atmosphere of mutual support, a group of strangers becomes a community of collaborators, an academic family within which creativity can take place, and students can work out what they are really interested in.

Year one in the studio

FP: A truly research-based education is something that delves into the unknown, is alive, and is constantly evolving. Uncertainty together with clarity is the key relationship here. It requires constant feedback, adjustment and dialogue between tutor and student. In many ways, it works like a musical instrument, rather than a machine that is operating under a set of predetermined instructions. Each instrument, player and performance is unique, cannot be repeated, and is dependent upon a huge number of external conditions.

When asked to lead the first year and to rethink what this stage of architectural education was about, I tried to remember everything I had done. At the same time, I was trying to be an innocent child, remembering nothing and imagining what I would like to have fun with if I were studying myself. Should we teach year-one architecture students all the fundamental skills that require a large chunk of our available time, or challenge their creativity and explore ways of being in the world? Should we focus our work on common sense, or encourage originality, questioning and imagination? Of course, balance is key here, so the intention was to incorporate both by teaching skills and knowledge as well as fun design and fabrication which might normally be considered too ambitious for year-one students.

In order to inspire students, we need to do all sorts of things that seem irrelevant to architecture: design a hat, do a dance, cook a meal, measure a river's flow, or analyse the way a donkey's tail swings to a Beethoven symphony. Prior to the building project, as a taster of what architecture is about, comes the installation project. Working together, we study a place, introduce an idea, explore possibilities, communicate with each other, get lost in a sea of options, find a driving design idea, fabricate, accomplish the project by meeting a precise deadline, work in the public domain and, finally, enjoy an evening of celebration with colleagues and guests. This project is described in detail in chapter five.

The main objective for the year is to teach students the essential requirements of how to design a building, as well as to inspire them to be ambitious, so that they can reinterpret definitions and stretch the boundaries to come up with something previously unimaginable. It is these magical moments of alchemy between tutors and students, when explorations and design experiments and ideas endlessly bounce back and forth, that is the unforgettable core and essence of a wonderful pedagogic model for a truly higher education.

The student of architecture has a lot to consider: personal dreams, skills, ideas, culture, life, human nature, politics, technology, and so on. The new architecture student is confronted with a need to learn the necessary making and drawing skills, but also to explore their own curiosity and build the confidence to communicate their ideas to strangers. This last part takes a long time to develop, build up and refine. Their relationship with the tutor is crucial at this formative and fragile stage. It requires a tutor who is confident and relaxed, as well as intense and ambitious; someone who encourages them to be daring and not to fear failure – after all, failing is the best way to ultimate success in years to come – and, above all, someone who is caring. They should be able to nudge them away from copying previous students' successful building designs and towards original thinking.

From the start, the core of my thinking when writing the curriculum has been to cultivate original thinking as a prelude to designing a building.

4.2

4.3

4.4

4.5

Students are, therefore, encouraged to mentally jump around different scales of projects and to oscillate between systematic, logical and patient analysis and quick intuitive responses. How does a feast – the installation in 1990 – help one understand human collective culture? This question has no clear answer, but the feast the students organised for this first installation project provided some indication. Delivering it required collaboration on many levels, between students, staff and college authorities, not to mention guests who were expected to move from point to point on a cold December night, and each course was planned for a particular space, adding another layer of interaction – in this case, between architecture and gastronomy. The outcome could not be predicted and the sense of suspense and excitement was a positive force. Throughout, the guests' expectations of food, service and space were constantly oscillating.

Architecture is not only designing walls. It is also about getting to the point where you know why, what and how, at which point you need to understand what a wall is: how can a wall not only divide and protect but at the same time enable opportunities for all sorts of possible activities to take place? How is the space of a wall understood in relation to the literal and figurative meanings of 'threshold'?

The interpretation of studio culture, outlined here, plays a particular part in initiating students into architectural education. So, how do we initiate them? Should their heads be in the clouds and their feet on the ground, or the other way around?

1. Present opportunities for students to think 'upside down', then help them rise on their own. Teach them to be creative and experimental.
2. Introduce a learning approach based on sharing ways of seeing the world, of thinking and discovering their own ways of understanding. Looking and seeing – observing creatively – is harder than design.
3. Spontaneity, intuition, and rational analysis go hand in hand. Quick and naive experimental models and drawings are often invaluable; the ugly model and the first ugly sketch can be foundations for later, refined design works. Students are encouraged to simultaneously think like curious five-year-old children as well as 65-year-old rational and systematic thinkers.
4. Teach basic architecture skills and ideas of developing mind and hand. Communication of ideas and stories is a priority, and a range of skills is needed that allow for conventional and inventive visual expression. Hand-drawing and hand-making skills are critical, as are a range of

digital skills. Nothing is more important than the constant dialogue between the mind and the hand.

5.   Each student is unique, so we as tutors have to adapt and design teaching to the individual's personal strengths, cultivate their interests and encourage self-analysis, so they bring their own culture into the communal year-one world. Students are encouraged to open up, reflect on their past life experiences and think about who they are.

6.   Both students and tutors must embrace and trust the unknown, and turn mistakes into inspiration. Risk-taking is key. They should learn that they do not know the 'answers'; that weird accidents often lead to phenomenal discoveries; when and how to obey the rules; and when to be a rebel. To do this, we must cultivate a culture of trust and a safe place where experiments are nurtured.

7.   The key qualities that an architecture student should develop are: personal memory, readiness, multitasking, improvisation, intuition and instinct.

8.   Students and tutors explore in parallel, learning from each other. This is the basis of research-based learning, which is the core of a design studio. The foundation of this partnership is skills of communication and a dialectic culture that enables students to express and develop their interests.

9.   Never give up! Perseverance and positive, open-minded stubbornness often lead to amazing revelations.

10.   Understand that there is no secret. It is hard work and unless you enjoy it, do not do it.

11.   Year-one studio culture should have its basis in real life and treat students as citizens with responsibilities for common causes, rather than spoon-feed them to produce lovely models and drawings. Treat students as equals to set ambition high. With this sense of value comes a sense of responsibility.

12.   Teamwork: only with team spirit, leadership, trust, and the ability to delegate can tutors and students achieve their visions.

The physical environment, with appropriate places and spaces for teaching, learning and practising architecture, is vital to encouraging a sense of idealism in new students. It also introduces them to realities, both of the profession and higher education. In-between spaces – lobbies, corridors, landings, windowsills and doorways – make a valuable contribution because they open up possibilities for informal contact and random thought, and, therefore, nurture a sense of obligation to make personal decisions.

In Wates House, we discovered that the corridors of an architecture school could act as internal street-like spaces with qualities, facilities and equipment that encourage all sorts of unplanned and unpredicted encounters. Walls can be lined with a collection of past students' drawings; shelves can store a diverse range of rough and final experimental models; a few tables can accommodate unplanned tutorials; and benches can facilitate resting, gossiping and modelmaking. Above all, these spaces can be used for sharing ideas and past experiences, and encourage a collective intimacy that helps first-year students to feel safe and confident. Personally, I have found that a lot of critical decisions and inspirational chats with colleagues and students happen 'on the way to the loo' or while making tea at the kitchen counter. Spontaneous activities — ephemeral in their nature, yet fundamental in the learning cycle as they allow students the freedom to improvise — are crucial.

Our corridors have witnessed events, tutorials, drawing, modelmaking, social encounters, interviews, and performances. If the walls had eyes and memory, films and operas would have been produced to share the stories and dreams that have taken place in these banal, yet magical, transitory spaces.

Experiencing the city

FP: Learning from the outside world is a huge part of year-one education, and is formally addressed by situating the installation project – described further in chapter five – in the public realm. Tutors should encourage students, on a daily basis, to experience the city: to visit relevant exhibitions, libraries, unimportant as well as famous buildings, construction sites, zoos, pubs, corner shops, cinemas, markets and special events, all of which contribute to their understanding of the role of an architect in the world. I would say that roughly a third of learning comes from studio life, a third from formal knowledge delivery, and a third from all the external activities mentioned above. In recent years, Bartlett students have volunteered in Accelerate's Open City programme, in which a diverse cohort of young people based in London is supported in developing an understanding of architecture and other disciplines of the built environment by participating in several skills workshops, amongst other activities, that prepare them to enter higher education. By helping to deliver these workshops, our students benefit from encouraging others to discover their real passions and interests, release their dormant creativities, try difficult and unfamiliar things, ask questions and have fun in making mistakes — all rare approaches in a secondary school classroom situation.

It is not only the tutors, lectures, workshops, books, exhibitions, courses and exposure to the world that are catalysts for learning. Beyond the skills and facilities that any institution provides, we should nurture the sense of belonging which gives students the confidence to question the establishment's status quo. We encourage them to question their preconceptions and to cultivate the sensibility, creativity and independence of thought that equips them to effectively search for and research new knowledge and be inventive. To achieve this, we rely heavily upon a studio culture that makes communication, exchange, sharing, and above all, trust, possible. In this way, we can support students to deal with the unknown, respond to change and cultivate their imagination.

Freedom and discipline

FP: Studio culture is possibly as important as delivery of teaching. The topography of our studio spaces, both private and collective, took many years to evolve and refine. Our aim is to make the studio an efficient space, whilst also allowing it to 'breathe' through unplanned events. Freedom and discipline are vital in this fragile learning environment. The inclusiveness of the open studio life is based upon its culture of trust and care. This environment should encourage the individual to have a distinct identity and develop his or her own interests and personality within a flexible and empathetic but clear frame. The more diverse the individuals, the more interesting the emerging alchemy of the group will be – this is one of the most fundamental concepts of studio culture. There is always a healthy tension between the individual student's learning modes versus the collective pressures of a studio ethos. This tension helps students understand that an architect has to multitask across various disciplines. One has to simultaneously be a poet, economist, cleaner, designer, maker, philosopher, surveyor, cook, mathematician and musician. As collective culture becomes increasingly rare in the outside world, the studio that nurtures collaboration and learning, in parallel with supporting students to develop their identities and interests, is invaluable.

4.6

4.7

Wates House

FP: Over the 23 years I spent working in the old Wates House – as The Bartlett's home at 22 Gordon Street was known before its recent transformation – the year-one studios and offices underwent numerous migrations. What was always a common rule was that a first-year student was given their personal space, as well as feeling that they were a part of the larger year-one ship. This was vital for the wellbeing, confidence, and development of the individual designer. Our third-floor studios and headquarters gradually developed into places where staff and students worked and learned in parallel. It is this unique nature of the architectural studio, which is simultaneously a place for learning and practice, where a truly research-based education can exist.

JEREMY MELVIN: On first sight, the old Wates House was an unpromising location to introduce first-year students to architectural education. It was aesthetically awful, cramped and prone to infestation and leaks, precisely the sort of building that one does not want students to design when they graduate. Yet, it was here that Pimenides had to take as the base and frame for creating a studio culture in which first-year students could begin to learn how to become architects. Despite appearances, Wates House was imbued with the characteristics of studio culture that became the underpinning and conceptual frame for Pimenides' teaching practice. It was a kind of conjuror's box with illusions beyond its physical limits, to places and ideas that form a skeletal diagram of the culture that architecture, and its studio culture, are a part of.

Successful studio culture has to be able to adopt and adapt to influences from almost any source, whether random guests or abandoned objects. To make these ideas and influences work, however, there has to be a frame of reference, just as surely as physical space needs physical structure. As we saw in chapter three, this metaphorical or allusive structure comes from fragments, seemingly random but actually carefully chosen and artfully placed on the floor, shelves, walls and various other surfaces. These serve to animate the literalness of the physical structure by posing the question of why an object might be selected and positioned in a particular place, but also by instigating a chain of thought to identify and understand an object and its positioning among others. Many of these questions would be unanswerable in literal terms but, by stimulating further questions, they start to build, if not a creative process itself, the mental building blocks of something akin to it.

What Wates House had was a sense of freedom. Almost every feature, nearly every space, was so inadequate for its purpose that it invited criticism, whether subliminal or overt. Nothing had to be treated as precious, nor did anything have any direct didactic value. The imagination could run free, unfettered by pre-existing and predetermined architecture that might limit what and how it was taught. The building became a kind of architectural 'degree zero'.[2] In these circumstances, any alteration was automatically an improvement and some tutors proved adept at making such interventions active teaching aids. For example, Patrick Weber, Pimenides' co-director between 2000 and 2014, was instrumental in forming the character of the teaching spaces and corridors by collaborating with students to manipulate and adorn the walls and ceilings. Freedom alone, though, is not enough. There also needs to be focus, both in the sense of specific spaces or localities – physical enablers and possibilities – within the building, where teaching and the social activities around it can take place and in the sense of what individuals, especially tutors and colleagues, can bring to shape the educational process.

The fantasy, the machine and the design

JM: At first sight, the idea of studio culture itself may seem vague, difficult and elusive, but Pimenides' concept of it draws deeply at the well of academic architectural theory and broader cultural history. In the sense put forward here, it is not just a tool for teaching but a manifestation of the position of architectural education within the culture of and discourse around architecture, and beyond that a depiction of how it might fit into a broader cultural context. In this sense, Pimenides' studio culture is part of her 'bearing witness to what it is to be an architect'.[3]

In his final essay, 'A Black Box: The Secret Profession of Architecture' (1990), Reyner Banham – UCL's first professor of architectural history – tried to define the role of the studio in teaching architects, a phenomenon that troubled him for almost 25 years.[4] For Banham, this black box is the system

---

2. Pimenides' practice sometimes, possibly subconsciously, echoes that of some recent and contemporary artists. One example is Robert Smithson, who was deeply interested in multi-layered interpretations of locations he carefully chose for his artworks, and for what is probably his most famous work, the *Spiral Jetty* (1970), he consciously wanted a context that stood outside any human-made conventions. In an article for *Landscape Architecture* he wrote: 'What is needed is an aesthetic method that brings together anthropology and linguistics in terms of building.' Quoted in Lynne Cooke, 'A Position of Elsewhere', *Robert Smithson: Spiral Jetty*, edited by Lynne Cooke and Karen Kelly, University of California Press, 2006, pp. 53–71. Originally published in Robert Smithson, 'A Thing Is a Hole in a Thing It Is Not', *Landscape Architecture*, vol. 58, no. 3, p. 205.
3. Jeremy Melvin and Bob Sheil, editors, *The Bartlett 175*, Architectural Review, 2016, p. 37.
4. Reyner Banham, 'A Black Box: The Secret Profession of Architecture', *A Critic Writes: Selected Essays by Reyner Banham*, edited by Mary Banham, Paul Barker, Sutherland Lyall and Cedric Price, University of California Press, 1997, pp. 292–99.

that produces architects. He identified an 'architectural mode' of producing buildings in the work of Hawksmoor and Soane, which could be contrasted with 'numerous other modes of designing buildings'.[5] This 'architectural mode,' he wrote, could be 'treated as a classic "black box", recognised by its output though unknown in its contents.'[6] The products of this black box – students – understand 'the fundamental value system on which architects operate... and the... assumptions on which it rests'. The studio, Banham states, is 'where architects are socialised into their profession'.[7]

For Banham, this is at least *unspoken* or even *unspeakable* but very real and self-evident. Naturally, 'as an outsider who was never socialised in the tribal long-house',[8] he was suspicious. By contrast, this chapter seeks a more benevolent interpretation of the mechanics of architectural education: opening up that 'black box', showing how and why it operates, and terming it 'studio culture' to suggest broader, more allusive and responsive attributes to architectural education than the term implies. Studio culture is partly fantasy, because if you cannot imagine a better world you should not be studying or teaching architecture; partly a machine, referring to teaching techniques rather than literal machines, that transforms fantasy into something discussable; and then something that has describable physical characteristics that we may call a design.

Donald Schön, in his book *The Reflective Practitioner: How Professionals Think in Action* (1983),[9] delves into the imperviousness of some professional discourses. In the fascinating analysis of a relationship between a graduate design student and tutor, Schön prises open the black box rather more than Banham could have anticipated. He establishes the social and historical context that led to the emergence of professions and shapes their position in society, summarised in the following generic exchange between a practitioner and academic: 'while I do not accept your view of knowledge, I cannot describe my own', an unpromising starting point to develop an 'epistemology of practice'.[10]

---

5. Wren, wrote Banham, could be 'clever' and 'inventive' in his buildings, though 'he was still not doing whatever it was that Hawksmoor had done to make great architecture out of as humdrum a concept as the interior of St Mary Woolnoth'. Banham, 'A Black Box', *A Critic Writes*, 1997, p. 292. The essay has numerous references to the studio, from which Banham as a non-architect clearly felt excluded. It is worth noting that Banham spent a year teaching in the then new Wates House before departing to continue his career in the US.
6. Banham, 'A Black Box', *A Critic Writes*, 1997, p. 293.
7. Banham, 'A Black Box', *A Critic Writes*, 1997, p. 298.
8. Banham, 'A Black Box', *A Critic Writes*, 1997, p. 296. Banham had studied art history at The Courtauld Institute of Art, completing a PhD with Nikolaus Pevsner, then worked for *The Architectural Review*, before being appointed to The Bartlett in 1964. He was an outsider in the sense of never being acculturated into the 'tribal longhouse' through being taught in the studio, but in almost every other sense he was an insider within the architectural community, though that did not suppress his iconoclastic approach.
9. Donald Schön, *The Reflective Practitioner: How Professionals Think In Action*, The Academic Publishing Group, 1991.
10. Schön, *The Reflective Practitioner*, 1991, p. 21. Developing an 'epistemology of practice' is part of Schön's aim.

Professions, he goes on to argue, are essential to modern society, whose members gain rights and privileges in return for vital specialist knowledge, which can also lead to abuse and calls for regulation. When specialist knowledge is applied by a practitioner, as opposed to an academic professional, it involves application of general principles from a large field and so the techniques become very important. Taken to its logical conclusion, Schön's thinking implies that these techniques can emerge, in part at least, under the umbrella of studio culture.

Some knowledge, Schön suggests, is based on hard science. The decline of positivism has led to a rebirth of interest in craft, artistry and myth. If technical rationality gives an incomplete picture of the world, reflective practitioners have to find other modes and registers to describe and communicate it. This is where his discussion of the tutorial relationship is relevant. Despite being the oldest recognised design profession, architecture has shifting boundaries. 'Drawing and talking are parallel ways of designing' Schön writes, '...and together make up what I call the language of designing.'[11] This is, of course, the typical dynamic in a design tutorial, where the interaction between student and tutor is largely verbal, but includes comments on the student's drawings and possibly sketches or diagrams drawn for instructive purposes by the tutor. Charting a series of tutorials between a student and tutor, Schön detects 'a gradual iteration to find a congruence of meaning' between them.[12] Gradually, as they become more confident with each other, their discussions become 'more elliptical to outsiders', precisely because they are moving deeper into a 'studio culture'.[13] This allows the tutor to have a body of knowledge that reframes the student's questions against a semi-objective, mutually understood base, which helps the student to understand their own intuitions, for example, oscillations between pure geometry and softened versions of it. On occasion, notes Schön, the tutor places this in terms of principles or in terms of external reference, for example other designers. In doing so, Schön shows that the process by which architects absorb their own culture need not be a black box, but can be made comprehensible by drawing on something like Pimenides' concept of studio culture.

11. Schön, *The Reflective Practitioner*, 1991, p. 80. On the importance of verbal language in design, see also Adrian Forty, *Words and Buildings: A Vocabulary of Modern Architecture*, Thames and Hudson, 2000, pp. 11–5.
12. Schön, *The Reflective Practitioner*, 1991, p. 81.
13. This interaction is described in Schön, *The Reflective Practitioner*, 1991, p. 81.

4.8

4.9

The studio as physical space

FP: Studio culture largely depends upon the character, facilities and qualities of the environment we work in. The physical space of architecture studios is a backdrop, scaffolding-frame and facilitator to design learning. In the life of an architecture student, learning happens in a classroom, at a personal working desk, outside, around a large table where group teaching occurs, in tight offices for consultations and in library corners where dreaming, through reading, can be discovered. All of these activities are possible if there is a certain degree of adaptability offered by the building. The character, scale, facilities and equipment should allow for very different approaches to architectural teaching. Nevertheless, there is some basic common ground and common-sense rules that should be followed. The ideal building would be a large warehouse space incorporating a whole range of quiet and private spaces; large internal and external spaces including walls that can accommodate temporary exhibitions; studios where intuitive and ad-hoc activities can take place; formal, dignified and accommodating spaces where students and staff present their work in crits; and a few social spaces where people mingle to eat and drink, where accidental encounters are encouraged. Students need to feel that they have their own place, not an impersonal space they occupy, that includes physical elements such as large collective tables, safe storage and 'pin-up' areas,[14] and a common room that has a bit of character and allows them to daydream, meet people from all parts of the school, or read a book quietly while having a break.

I never imagined that the character and the topography of an architecture school would be so influential on studio culture and people. Our former buildings – Wates House and the temporary home at 140 Hampstead Road – were full of life and excitement. Both were unique in the sense that you could improvise within them. If the studios were too cramped, in two days you erected a plywood wall. It was not always comfortable — people had to hustle, squeeze and make things work — but that is probably what made possible the atmosphere of creativity. The buildings were full of temporary objects and walls, which created focused 'pods' within a collective space.

There is a danger in any consciously designed studios that they could be too prescribed and inflexible to be susceptible to the sort of adjustment described above. In many ways, this adjustment is more important than pristine and perfect design because it definitively invites students to become

---

14. Where students can pin their work to the walls to present, look at or discuss it.

reflective of their surroundings and to experiment with improving them. When the spaces meet many of the expectations of 'design quality', students can be either unmotivated or intimidated, reducing the scope of their creative energies. As we have seen, it is important that they feel at home in their studio spaces and comfortable enough, not just to work but also to socialise, daydream and read. All of this is greatly facilitated if they feel that they have had some agency in creating the character of those spaces.

What is on our walls is also crucial to our learning environments. The issue of providing elements of inspiration and not simply work that can be copied or mimicked is a critical aspect of education. A student put it beautifully: 'it is healthy to walk along a corridor with walls holding material that jumps into your mind when you encounter them daily'.[15] It is almost like an orchestra or a puppet theatre, where specific figures escape their context and start an intimate dialogue with you. Louis Kahn wrote about the potential for such spaces to enable different kinds of learning to take place, especially between peers: 'There could be a gallery instead of a corridor. The gallery is really the classroom of the students' in which the student 'who didn't quite get what the teacher said' could talk to a fellow student 'who seems to have a different kind of ear, and they both could understand.'[16]

JM: The studio in which studio culture emerges can be considered as manifested, or at least an analogy of certain physical phenomena. These include the table as an analogue of an urban square; the office and consulting room as a boudoir or votary space; and the places where crits happen as sites for specialised interaction. Each of these is primarily physical but, in parallel, is a series of phenomena that is more elusive and metaphorical: fantasy, machine and reality. What makes the notion of studio culture so powerful, if complicated, is that each element is inter-related.

FP: The prime physical enabler in The Bartlett's first-year studio culture is a big, more or less square, table placed near the centre of a large space. Empty or full, the table immediately draws the eye towards it. It should be hospitable and inviting, but formal. In 30 years, three tables have been anchors for collective and individual learning. What is common to these tables is that they are freestanding and large enough to accommodate big and messy events, as well as enabling private moments around their edges.

---

15. Ruth Allan, first year student 2001-2, in conversation with Pimenides, February 2016.
16. Louis Kahn, *Conversations with Students*, Princeton University Press 1969, p 34. The book was compiled from conversations between Kahn and students at Rice University, Houston.

4.11

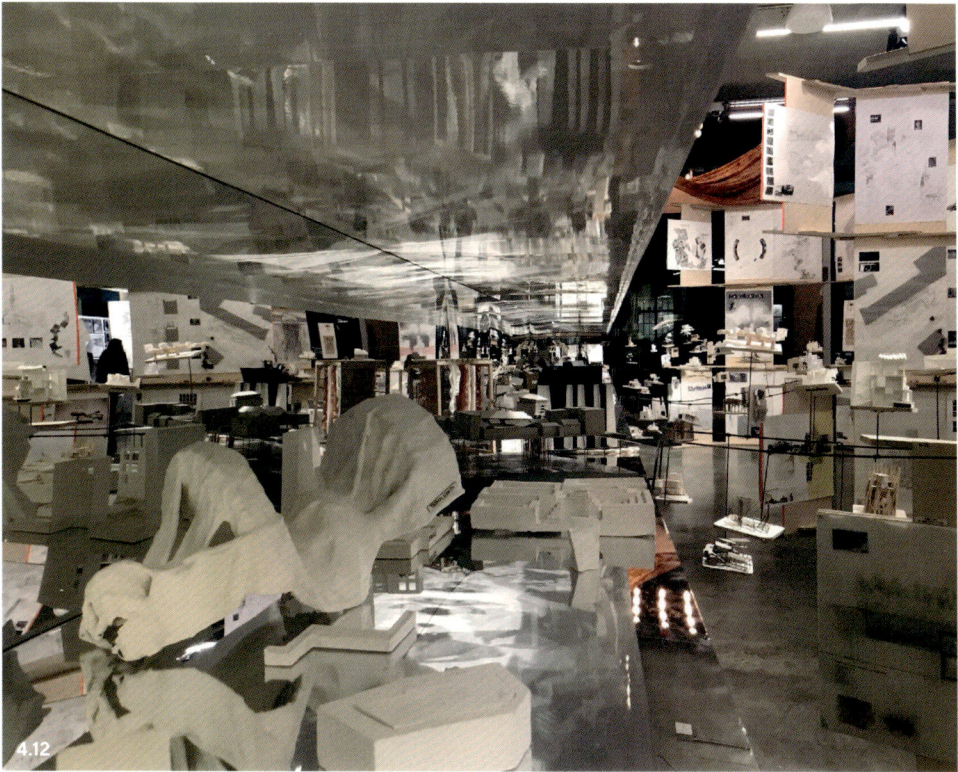

4.12

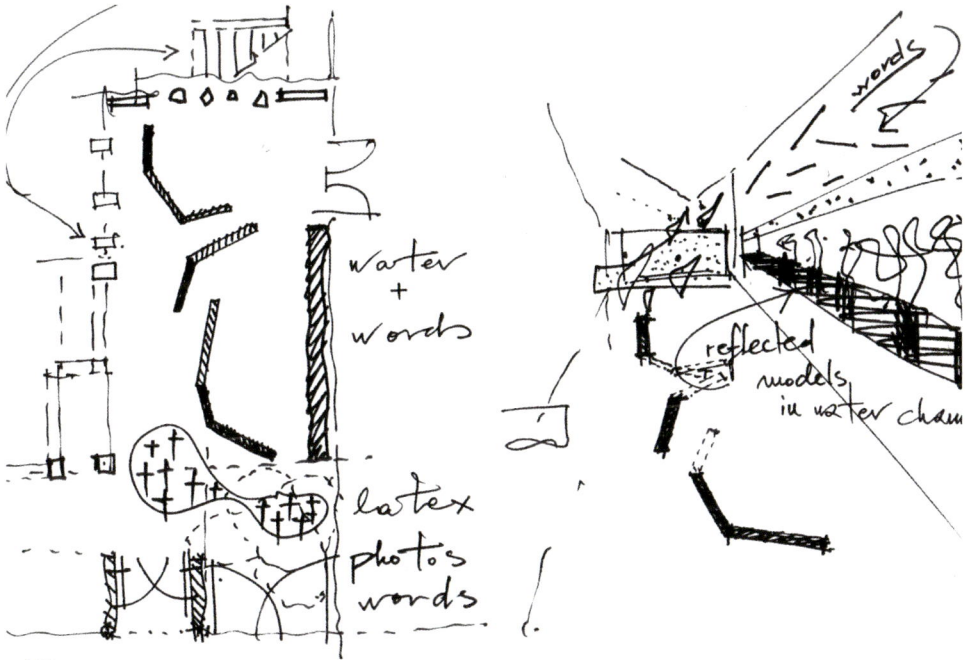

water
+
words

latex
photos
words

words

reflected
models
in water cham

4.13

The glass table in the old Wates House staff office remembers a lot of events: marking, formal dinners, informal chats, using its transparent surface to trace drawings, seminars, storage and interviews. The table was picked up for very little money from an auction in North London and takes 12 people to move it; even on a material level it serves as a reference point for stability, versatility and collective culture. The second table, a Victorian timber library table, has four vast, beautifully carved legs; it is robust but also delicate. The multiple scars and marks on the surface are a diary of all the lives and events that it has accommodated. In our new building, the main tool of our collective culture is a 15-metre-long, multi-coloured, Peter Cook-designed table. It can accommodate, in a highly inventive manner, all sorts of activities: personal study, tutorials, large meals, workshops and desk crits. One precedent for this was the large square kitchen table in the house of the distinguished architect, Richard Burton and his wife Mireille – parents of The Bartlett's former workshop co-manager Bim Burton.[17] Its multiple purposes included entertaining, feeding and on occasion acting as a work surface, for different groups of people: family, friends, work colleagues and community groups. At an underlying level, what unites all these examples is that the table and its many manifestations are a way of generating, inducing, expressing and developing ideas. In this way, the table takes on many of the characteristics of a city square,[18] where communication can draw on all the senses: sight, touch, taste, smell and sound. Perhaps easier to achieve in a semi-public building such as a university, it can also bring together some of the basic stimuli that feed into architecture.

City squares, though, have limits, and so does the teaching studio. There are the physical limits of walls, floor and ceiling and also doors of entering and leaving. Doors are very important. If closed they signify privacy, but opening them is an invitation to serendipitous contact with other colleagues who may be engaged in completely different teaching programmes. The value of a door is that it gives someone the choice of being part of or isolated from noise and activity. It allows a rich mixture of activities to coexist. We might remember that in ancient Greek, *diádromos* does not mean only corridor but passage, as well as journey. By facilitating visual

17. Richard Burton (1933–2017). See Louis Kahn on tables, *Conversations with Students*, p. 59. For an appreciation of the Burton House see Richard Burton and James O. Davies, *An Extra Dimension: The Burton House Modern Architecture in the Making*, Right Angle Publishing, 2015.
18. Richard Sennett's attempt to describe the interactive and communicative nature of public space in his book *The Conscience of the Eye: The Design and Social Life of Cities*, Faber & Faber, 1990, offers some insight into this condition. As he writes in the introduction, the book aims 'at relating architecture, urban planning, public sculpture and the visual scenes of the city to its cultural life' (p. xiv). Pimenides' conception of studio culture proposes a parallel to this, exploring how the creation of architecture (including urban planning, and through installations, reaching as far as public sculpture) draws on and contributes to cultural life.

contact and spatial proximity, these spaces can contribute to the studio culture. The central table is surrounded by edges, which are less focused and well defined than the people and thoughts around it, but nonetheless provide sustenance.[19]

The office-home

FP: Alongside the table – the square – and the design studio itself, two other physical spaces are essential to studio culture: the office and the crit space. Both are very different to the table's sense of welcome, as they have a structured relationship – the door – with the space beyond. In Wates House there were two linked offices, one something of an annex to the other, whose primary occupants were staff. This allowed for a rich variety of spatial arrangements, and spaces were equally adaptable to private discussion, group tutorials, somewhere to assemble portfolios for review and also where accidental encounters happened, such as when colleagues or visitors dropped in for tea.

As we saw in chapter three, the office is a space for collective teaching, discussing ideas, debating, planning future projects, all sorts of events related to year one, interviews, tutoring and private discussion. Even more so, it represents a little space where students and staff can find something different from the public anonymity of the studios, corridors, the university, and London. Perhaps it can offer a sense of belonging; it is a quiet, safe space within which we can retreat from the exposure of public academic life, and where we can get lost in the physical or imaginary world.

Over a period of 30 years this office has evolved and migrated. It started as a humble corner off the south corridors of Wates House, where it was initially filled with notes, materials, and salvaged old leaded-oak doors from the original Friends' House nearby; later emigrating to the second floor and then the third, where its existence and role was rather modest and minimal. In 2000, year one ascended to the third floor of Wates House and an office was gradually established off the north third-floor corridor. The combination of that small office, our year-one office, the central common-room-style meeting space and the individual studios established a unique home for our collective studio culture.

---

19. Orchestral conductor Gustavo Dudamel gave an insight into musical education, when he argued that including young musicians on the periphery of the stage, during a performance, can be an invaluable experience; the honour and trust that this gesture involves will inspire and inform them with an experience that would help them on the road in becoming musicians later in life. Dudamel shared these thoughts after a great performance with young children, prior to blowing out candles on his birthday cake at St Luke's, Old Street, London, 2011.

4.14

4.15

4.16

4.17

4.18

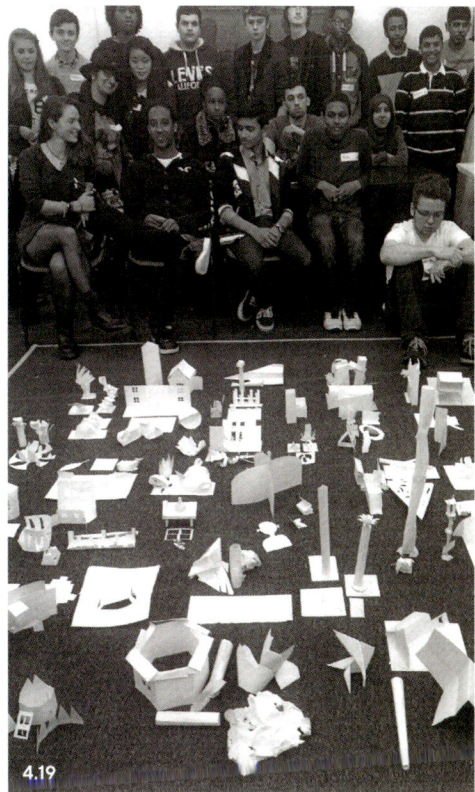

4.19

Next, came our temporary Hampstead Road space, where we were based for three years, with an openness and large scale that offered a unique and experimental atmosphere. Finally, fate brought us back to the refurbished Wates House, 22 Gordon Street, where the current 'office-home' can be found on the fifth floor, acting as an annexe to our sixth-floor studios above.

Culture within a wider system of culture

JM: Certain spaces, when charged with ritual, memory, decoration, ornament and enticing spatial and formal arrangements, can appear to evoke something other than their physical limits or functions; something that is not possible in modern scientific terms but which stimulates the imagination within a frame of reference we might call 'culture'. In this sense, studio culture is a special framework within a wider system of culture.

The objects in Pimenides' office all have some relevance to studio culture and the experience of 30 years spent teaching first-year students with and through it. Some refer to projects and programmes from previous years, which themselves connect to the sites that were set or the objects that were studied, represented by photographs, drawings, models or casts. Among them are other images and shapes, such as the monastery of an early Christian foundation in Athens, that adds another cultural layer which constitutes the city's deep history.[20] These carry some classical notions into the present day, such as the Ancients' belief that the Oracle's Temple at Delphi was at the centre of the world. This may be nonsense in light of modern physics and geology, but as a persistent belief it has something to offer to anyone trying to teach or learn how to infuse a design for a place with significance beyond its physical existence and literal function.

It could be claimed that this sort of transcendence is the essence of architecture or, in Banham's words, 'the architectural mode of making buildings'.[21] It certainly was so for Abbot Suger, the designer and commissioner of the first Gothic building, the Abbey of St Denis (1145), a French royal shrine on the outskirts of Paris. He justified the lavish

---

20. For Louis Kahn, all architectural phenomena are somehow connected: 'An architect is part of the treasury of architecture to which the Parthenon belongs, the Pantheon belongs...' and in joining architects become 'an offering to architecture'. Kahn, *Conversations with Students*, 1969, p. 53. In *The Conscience of the Eye*, Sennett discusses how its precursor, *The Fall of Public Man*, 1979, noted 'how the public realm lost its life when it lost these rituals', i.e. the rituals that characterised public behaviour and distinguished public from private lives (p. xiv). On the way rituals contain memories of past events or beliefs, see for example, George Hersey, *The Lost Meaning of Classical Architecture*, The MIT Press, 1988.
21. See Banham, 'A Black Box', *A Critic Writes*, 1997. Ludwig Wittgenstein famously opined, 'Architecture immortalises or glorifies something. Hence there can be no architecture where there is nothing to glorify'. Ludwig Wittgenstein, *Culture and Value*, edited by G. H. von Wright, Blackwell, 1998, p. 74e.

expenditure and sumptuous appearance of the abbey, often cited as the first fully gothic building because it simultaneously glorified both the saints whose relics it held and France itself – Denis being the patron saint of the French people – where Suger was chief minister. The art historian Erwin Panofsky both translated Suger's writings and analysed his motives and thinking in his essay 'Abbot Suger of St Denis', from which the following discussion draws.[22]

Panofsky argues that Suger was motivated to write an explanation of the building and artefacts at St Denis to justify them and especially to divert the wrath of the notoriously argumentative and puritanical abbot St Bernard of Clairvaux. In this exercise Panofsky was greatly helped by the writings of the so-called Dionysius, (i.e. Denis), the Pseudo-Areopagite, a Christian Neo-Platonist who lived in the late fifth or early sixth century CE. The abbey held his manuscripts in the belief – later thought to be mistaken – that they were the work of the titular patron, who imbued them with a particular authority for Suger.

They also, suggests Panofsky, held another attraction for Suger: 'In accepting what he took as the *ipse dixits* [the things he himself said] of Saint Denis, Suger did homage to the patron saint of his abbey but also found the most authoritative confirmation of his innate beliefs and proclivities'.[23] So, according to Panofsky, Suger's mistaken belief in the manuscripts coming from the hand of the abbey's patron saint, gives the idea they expressed a unique authority, which linked text, building and the state of France. This also supported his aesthetic preferences, in essence that light emanating from the divine would pick out and beautify artfully shaped matter, for example art and artefacts, which gave them divinely ordained purpose. The argument led to one of Suger's best known passages:

Thus, when – out of my delight in the beauty of the House of God – the loveliness of the many-coloured gems has called me away from external cares, and worthy meditation has induced me to reflect, transferring that which is material to that which is immaterial... I see myself dwelling, as it were, in some strange region of the universe which neither exists entirely in the slime of the earth nor entirely within the purity of heaven...[24]

22. Abbot Suger, *On the Abbey Church of St-Denis and Its Art Treasures*, edited, translated and annotated by Erwin Panofsky, Princeton University Press, 1948; and Erwin Panofsky, *Meaning in the Visual Arts*, Penguin, 1993, pp. 155–80.
23. Panofsky, *Meaning in the Visual Arts*, 1993, p. 165.
24. Suger, *On the Abbey Church of St-Denis and Its Art Treasures*, 1948, pp. 64–5 partially quoted in Panofsky, *Meaning in the Visual Arts*, 1993, p. 162.

Rarely has the case for art's transcendence been so eloquently expressed. While avoiding these theological connotations, Pimenides' practice operates with a sense that through illusion and allusion, certain individual instances can appear to reach beyond their positions in a Newtonian concept of space and time.

In bringing together various existing architectural forms and devices into one coherent style at St Denis, Suger inaugurated a new phase of the Western architectural tradition. He also inaugurated new possibilities for architectural expression and ways of interpreting it. Gothic has been interpreted as the architectural counterpart to Scholastic theology,[25] of which one of the cornerstones, the fourfold method of interpretation, has some application. The leading Scholastic philosopher, St Thomas Aquinas, adapted this intellectual device with roots in ancient classical thought as a technique of biblical exegesis. The affinity alluded to here, though, is not about Gothic as such, but about the different levels of meaning and significance that Pimenides traces in studio culture.

Dante Alighieri, though primarily a poet, had distinct philosophical interests, and was the first writer to suggest, a generation or so after Aquinas, that the fourfold method of interpretation could be applied to secular as well as biblical contexts.[26] The Bible's divine origins, previous commentators had argued, made its stories uniquely capable of carrying the intellectual load of four levels of meaning.[27] Dante's own poetry, he believed, came from divinely inspired visions, and so, while not canonically biblical, shared divine origin.

The relevance of this to Pimenides' concept of studio culture is perhaps not immediately obvious and so needs some explanation. The first stage is to outline the fourfold method; the second is to indicate how, in the formulation of one of Dante's recent commentators, William Anderson, he used it as one of several analytical techniques and intellectual structures to give coherence and purpose to his work, especially *The Divine Comedy* (1308-20); and the third is to show an affinity with Pimenides' notion of studio culture. The following comments are indebted to the chapter 'The Six Guides and the Four Levels of Meaning' in Anderson's book *Dante the Maker* (1980).[28]

---

25. See, for example – at opposite ends of the spectrum of intellectual accessibility –John Summerson, 'Heavenly Mansions' (1946), *Heavenly Mansions and Other Essays on Architecture*, W. W. Norton & Company, 1963, pp. 1–28, and Erwin Panofsky, *Gothic Architecture and Scholasticism*, The Archabbey Press, 1951.
26. Dante explained his interpretation of the fourfold method in his letter to Can Grande della Scala, ruler of Verona and patron of Dante, especially paragraphs 7–35. This has been reproduced and translated many times, and is available online, at https://faculty.georgetown.edu/jod/cangrande.english.html.
27. William Anderson, *Dante the Maker*, Hutchinson, 1983, p. 329.
28. Anderson, *Dante the Maker*, 1983, pp. 320–45.

The fourfold method has roots in ancient classical thought but evolved in the hands of late Christian thinkers. It received a further and decisive boost in the Middle Ages through the Scholastics, including Aquinas. Essentially, it holds that stories and perhaps objects have literal and allegorical meanings. The fourfold method comes from the belief that allegorical meaning could be split into three further levels: the purely allegorical, the moral and the anagogic. In this context, allegorical meaning relates to the broader social significance of the phenomenon under consideration; the moral level to its significance for the individual, especially for Christian thinkers, the personal journey towards divine grace; and the anagogic meaning to the achievement and condition of that state of grace. Importantly, each level is dependent on the others, even if not everyone may be able to follow them entirely.

Anderson shows how Dante applies this method to develop *The Divine Comedy*'s intellectual structure, along with various other philosophical and literary techniques. This provides an intellectual frame for his work, which relates it to both the classical and Christian traditions, and, crucially, a synthesis between the two. It was this goal to which Dante orientated much of his intellectual effort, and it finds expression in his encounter with the soul of the Emperor Constantine in the sixth canto, the third part 'Paradise'. As the emperor who began the Christianisation of the Roman Empire, Constantine epitomises the union that Dante sought.[29]

Why, then, is this arcane and esoteric piece of Medieval thought relevant to Pimenides' teaching practice, and studio culture in particular? Pimenides is not a keen scholar of Dante so this can only be answered by showing affinities between the two. It is tempting, but hardly definitive, to note that the *Comedy* starts with Dante wandering in a state of confusion in a dark wood, where he faces perils, until he detects the shade of Virgil – the first of the six guides in Anderson's chapter title – who starts to guide him through various challenges on the arduous route to Paradise. Relating this to Pimenides' description of the challenge facing students at the start of their first year does not require an enormous imaginative leap.

Moreover, the whole *Comedy*, whatever techniques of analysis might be used – the fourfold method or any other – to understand it, is about an individual who, through a long and difficult journey and encounters with people, visions, ideas and, maybe, objects, achieves a 'state of grace'. The concept of a state of grace may now be anachronistic, and it is certainly

---

29. It might be stated the relationship between religious and political power is one of the central aspects of Western thought, at least from late antiquity until the Enlightenment of the 18th century.

not implied here that students reach it through some form of educational experience. Rather than a state of grace though, the goal might be stated as enabling students to become 'reflective practitioners' (Donald Schön's phrase); that is, they become aware of themselves and social implications of their capabilities, where they are able to reflect on their personal experience and enthusiasm in a way that allows them to recognise the value of what they already know and to use it as a basis to develop their skills as an architect.[30]

This is possible because the underlying tribulations of life, as depicted in the odyssey, depend on a coherent whole, which Dante believed to emanate from, and whose coherence depended on God, which might not be commonly accepted now. Again, though, it is possible to find an affinity with the journey through studio culture and Dante through the realm of the dead. Its structure sets up possibilities for students to encounter different ideas, people, sites, buildings and objects, through which they have to navigate their own way, with tutors often less prescriptive than Virgil to help. Studio culture is, too, a vision, though it may also have real existence that, whatever apparent contradictions it may introduce to students, stems from what is ultimately a coherent intuition of architecture and its purposes. Through it, in interaction with their own personalities and individual interests, students can discover and develop enormous variety and a broad scope for them to express.

From a different perspective, there is also an affinity between the fourfold method and the inherent nature of architecture. Architecture is rooted in a literal level, which might have meaning but is perhaps best described as function. Works of architecture may also aspire to allegorical significance, which lies beyond, but may grow out of, function. That allegorical significance can also be broken down further into the allegorical proper or social significance; and the moral, or significance for the individual. The anagogic or spiritual level is more controversial, but it might be suggested that a few buildings reach it.[31]

30. As the American postmodern architect and educator Charles W. Moore put it in his essay 'Eleven Agonies and One Euphoria': 'Euphoria: With all the absurdities of a strict professional education in architecture in a changing world, we have in our province the process of design: that combination of research and understanding and intuition and improvisation which tries out solutions to problems in too many unknowns to be susceptible of solution by the disciplines based on logic and words. The complicated work is in desperate need of the ministrations of the designer, not the arrogant visionary who slaps preconceptions onto the unwilling, but the solver of the loosely structured problems, the visionary who dares to destroy constructive preconceptions to come to solutions he has to invent (and which he is willing to test, with the people with whom and for whom the solutions are made). The world needs this desperately. If we can lose the agonies attending our professional hang-ups... we will have left in our province one of the key tools for the solution of the world: design. And from this we can take heart'. Charles W. Moore, *You Have to Pay for the Public Life: Selected Essays of Charles W. Moore*, edited by Kevin Keim, The MIT Press, 2001, p. 166.
31. Pimenides' descriptions of the temple at Delphi and Sydney Opera House in chapter 2 suggest they might come close, though everyone would have their own list.

Finally, the fourfold method starts with something concrete and tangible or, at least, possible to perceive through the senses. Intellect, imagination and faith then operate on it to reach further levels of meaning. Anderson cites the theologian Hugh of Saint Victor's injunction that before a student tries to discover the allegorical meanings of Noah's Ark they should first attempt to mentally visualise the 'physical details of the ark and its building' to 'see and experience it as a three-dimensional construction'.[32] Pimenides might echo that sentiment in introducing students to the objects in her office or indeed to the sites she sets for projects.

It should be repeated that this is not a conscious element in Pimenides' conception of studio culture. What is suggested here though is that her conception has strong affinities with the fourfold method. Furthermore, as indicated above, the fourfold method is close to the core of European culture. Through influences like her tutors Joseph Rykwert and Dalibor Vesely and her family, especially her grandfather Nikos Manthos, as well as her own interests, Pimenides has been exposed to that tradition. There is also a case, as set out above, to suggest that the fourfold method has a particular application to architecture.

The proposition that studio culture may evince and evoke systems of ideas and spaces that lie far beyond the literal confines of the building is not as far-fetched as Newtonian physics or the reductivist side of modernist architectural thinking one might assume. The studio itself, the table, crit space and especially the office with its fragments, could become places where the imagination comes out of itself, interacts with other ideas and intuitions, and reassembles into a physical existence charged with other levels of meaning.

The crit space

FP: The review or crit space should be a formal, graceful and dignified place, where all sorts of dialogues, conversations, debates, and the formal exchange of ideas, knowledge and designs can take place. To clearly and critically debate and converse, one needs a quiet, well-lit environment that is, most of all, a neutral, calm, inspiring and uplifting place. How can this space provide a forum for creative debate, presenting work as well as ideas?

---

32. Anderson, *Dante the Maker*, 1983, p. 335. Anderson gives a reference in his bibliography to Aelred Squire, *Hugh of Saint-Victor: Selected Spiritual Writings*, Nabu Press, 2011, pp. 60–72.

JM: The end point of a student project is the crit, which is staged in the third spatial condition of the studio: the crit space. Theatrical and stimulating, the crit is common in creative education. A nuanced depiction of the architecture school crit and the space in which it occurs comes from Louis Kahn in *Conversations with Students* (1969).[33] Asked to comment on how a school of architecture might be designed, he states that 'every building must have a sacred space', and then asks (and answers):

What is the sacred space in a school of architecture? It could be the lobby or the space where you gather together for reaction. Reaction to your work means approval of millions, even though only a few are present. It's the kind of thing in which you can believe, and that is a tremendous thing.

This, he argues, is the crit space, in his words, the 'jury room... a room where you meet for a kind of review of an experience in doing a building... starting with a piece of white paper'.[34] A classroom might be like 'Jackson Pollock with paint on the floor' but the crit space has to be a sanctuary from the noise of the rest of the studio or school.[35]

For Kahn, the crit space is the culmination of the educational experience, giving back to students an intellectual structure of belief, derived from their own projects, which in turn emerge from briefs, and all the while nurtured by the predominant studio culture. By drawing together all these strands from different positions into one place, and one moment (the crit itself), that place becomes a sacred one.[36]

The office is a vital element in the 'machine' that, together with fantasy and reality, constitutes part of studio culture. Here, the subjective fantasies of individual students are drawn out through one-to-one tutorials and calibrated with the fragments that line the room. These fragments are so numerous, and offer so many different interpretations, that students can pick one or more which they sense might fit with their private ideas. These subjective thoughts then join into a relationship, however loose and attenuated, with the constellation of ideas, images and objects already in their heads. We explore the role of fragments further in the eponymous chapter.

---

33. Kahn, *Conversations with Students*, 1969.
34. Kahn, *Conversations with Students*, 1969, pp. 64–5.
35. Kahn, *Conversations with Students*, 1969, pp. 65–6.
36. Kahn, *Conversations with Students*, 1969, p. 66.

In the process described above, the essential tool is the project brief or, as Kahn put it, 'the rewriting of programming'.[37] It brings focus to a specific architectural task to which all students have to respond. This also interacts with the students' subjective ideas and requires them to shape them. It follows that developing and setting a brief is a formidable task because it must be sufficiently wide for any student to engage with, but defined in such a way that the teaching purpose can be achieved. It can do that in part by referring to the material – fragments – in the office, suggesting links between them and the place and purpose of the project, and inviting the students to speculate and imagine based on this foundation.

FP: The life of a school of architecture is more dynamic and important than the structure of the building itself. The flexibility of the building will offer the possibility of daily life to evolve and develop. We need to feel that we can make a mess to fully experience the vibrant and experimental life of the school.

Studio culture is a complex web of people and spirit, which can be seen most profoundly through the many Bartlett migrations, from Wates House to the blank canvas of Hampstead Road, then back to Gordon Street and its rebuilt home. Each wave of people dealt with the excitement of change, the excitement of the unknown, and the excitement of hope. A film by Squint Opera described the life and transition between the three buildings.[38] In it, the school's director, Bob Sheil, points out:

Change ultimately is the most powerful creative force; and this is something we have always talked about in the abstract; it exists on paper, it exists in a model but we are now going through it ourselves physically and I think that it is going to be an incredibly powerful experience for the school.

The value of change in studio space is communicated by a past student, Rosie Murphy:

Everyone [at Hampstead Road] is changed in some way. But it is beautiful what we do. And when we get stressed, it is about a drawing and it is about a model, feeling safe and protected here from the harsh realities of the outside world. So a bit of perspective is what we have gained from all these years: people change, thoughts change and we are in what I think is a really unique

37. Kahn, *Conversations with Students*, 1969, p. 55.
38. Squint Opera, 'Transition' 2017

moment in time, whether it is within our school or within the world. Change needs to happen; we now have the opportunity to decide what happens next, what goes next, because we are not fixed; and when there is instability there is also excitement.[39]

Another ex-student, Arthur Harmsworth, commented upon the value of the warehouse-like, large volume, studio where everybody was encouraged to mix:

There is a lot more integration between the units. ... That kind of meshing is really interesting because different units have different styles. You can see everyone else work, anything that catches your attention, really you are encouraged to go over and look at it and talk to the person working on it.[40]

As we have seen, we need to provide facilities but not give complete spaces; students benefit from collective spaces but we also need to allow each individual to collect, assemble and develop their own personality. I cannot think of better advice for us when we entered our new building at 22 Gordon Street than Peter Cook's comment: 'there should be no dividing line between teaching a piece of building, exhibiting, drawing... architects should not hide in an academic area: I think they should be out there.'[41]

We have seen how beyond the basic environment and facilities of, for example, a desk pencil, chair, book, building a collective culture in our studio-based architectural family is of critical value. To be inspired and creative you should feel safe, left alone, that you belong to a place but also have the freedom to be who you are. The physical qualities of a studio are catalysts for the culture to grow from it. The space has to be adaptable to adjust to a range of situations and activities. Studio culture can be compared to an octopus, with tentacles that have the capacity to address various objects and phenomena. It expands and extends well beyond the studio walls, reaching out towards other relationships and locations in the city and beyond. It is largely dependent upon a number of people that contribute to and believe in this collective effort, enabling students to flourish individually but within the framework of safety, inspiration, collaboration and the challenge of a multifaceted way of learning and living.

39. Rosie Murphy, speaking in autumn 2014.
40. Arthur Harmsworth, speaking in winter 2015.
41. Peter Cook, comments made at the opening of an exhibition to mark his 80th birthday at The Bartlett, February 2017.

Chapter 4 images
Photographs courtesy of Frosso Pimenides unless otherwise stated.

4.1 A frieze of doodles by student Lydia Xynogala produced for the end-of-year exhibition, capturing students' time in studios and field trips. 5 x 100cm, pen on white card, June 2001.
Photo: Robert Newcombe.

4.2 & 4.3 A team of students collaborating during the last installation at Pitzhanger Manor – available wall surfaces, a central table, and flexibility of space are key in enabling studio culture to exist – November 2014. Photo: Bartlett Architecture BSc year-one archive.

4.4 The year-one staff room wall, off the main studio central meeting and working space. Pimenides describes 'fragments of old installations, end of year exhibitions, and full-scale material explorations, skilfully arranged by my then co-director Patrick Weber', Wates House. Photo: Robert Newcombe.

4.5 A typical end-of-year tea party in Gordon Square, June 1994. Students with then-co-director of year one Graeme Sutherland, Frosso Pimenides, Mark Hayduk, and Gill Scampton. Photo: Bartlett Architecture BSc year-one archive.

4.6 The year-one staff room teaching studio, described by Pimenides as 'an anchor for staff and students'. She continues: 'it provided us all with a sense of collective culture and belonging, and acted as an invaluable resource for archiving books and models that were used daily in our teaching. It allowed us to have private meetings with the students and staff; it hosted exams, group tutorials, fabrication workshops, interviews and lunches. A long working counter, a huge central table and masses of shelving enabled that culture to exist.'

4.7 The first ever Summer Show, Wates House, June 1991. Photo: Bartlett Architecture BSc year-one archive.

4.8 A regular weekly working crit during a group installation project. The studios were able to host group tutorials, fabrication, debates, and individual study. Including: Brian O'Reilly, Abi Abdolwohabi, Emmanouil Stavrakakis, Frosso Pimenides with then-co-director Nat Chard. 134 Hampstead Road studios, October 2014.

4.9 Exploring sectional drawing through dissecting fruit; an annual part of the year-one media studies programme, an element of the Architecture BSc programme.

4.10 Fresh fruit, dissected: 'in a few days, the fruits were magically transformed into the most unpredictable 3D objects, a great resource for study'.

4.11 'One of the most beloved evenings for staff and students is when the UCL Portico is annually transformed into the best dance floor in town during the annual Summer Show opening party. This place connects to the city and the skies in a totally surreal manner.'

4.12 Year-one exhibition space at the Summer Show, June 2019.

4.13 Exploratory sketches for the exhibition space by Frosso Pimenides, April 2019.

4.14 Year-one exhibition space, June 2015. A timber armature – designed and manufactured by Emmanuel Vercruysse and students – served the double purpose of holding student models, as well as representing the footprint of the Thames Pathway. Recipient of the Show Opener's Prize, awarded by Carme Pinós.

4.15 A barbecue in the yard at 140 Hampstead Road, organised by Indigo Rohrer, Tim Lucas and Frosso Pimenides.

4.16 Students in The Bartlett's B-made workshop at Hampstead Road, where the installation pieces for the procession project were slowly taking shape, December 2016.

4.17 Media studies plaster-casting day with Joel Cady.

4.18 Robert Newcombe running a family workshop at 22 Gordon Street, part of The Bartlett Summer Show, June 2019. Photo: Bartlett communications team.

4.19 Open City, Accelerate workshop studying places around Bloomsbury. Wates House, Spring 2014.

5.1

Chapter 5: Installations

Dreaming and building: the annual installation project

FROSSO PIMENIDES: Every autumn term since 1990 has culminated in a group installation project, where all students and staff collaborate on design research and fabrication. It is the first attempt to bring together the various factors that make up architectural education, and is a vital component in building a collective culture and a form of 'academic family', where friendships and a level of trust emerge amongst students that will last for the duration of their studies, possibly even a lifetime.

I came up with this six-week project back in 1990. Each year the teaching team explores options for a new theme and location, writes the programme, and organises and initiates this collective working culture. We introduce students to various fabrication techniques and new ways of looking at things around us, and we teach various skills and explore ideas together. The project provides an opportunity for students to experience 'thinking through making'. It culminates with a celebratory event, often open to the public, in mid-December. This is a collaborative, demanding and vital part of our pedagogic programme in which we start to expand the territories of what architecture addresses, challenge students' preconceptions and help them to look afresh at the world. The exchange of ideas and skills, informed by students' cultural backgrounds, is enabled through the collective spirit of the installation project. Students, divided into around nine groups, embark upon a long journey that prompts them to consider their role as citizens and their responsibility to our planet and to each other. We develop their independence of mind and their confidence, and we see various forms of research by design emerge.

The installation project also gives students essential experience for the end of the year when they are asked to demonstrate that they can invent a programme for a real place and situation, for which they imagine and design a building. At that point they have to situate it in a real context, which they have surveyed beforehand, write the brief, design, resolve structural and

5.2

5.3

5.4

environmental issues, and represent it through a range of abstract and precise models, photos and drawings. Finally, they communicate their design and ideas to a panel of critics and tutors. The installation project introduces each of these tasks to the students a few months earlier in the course.

In this chapter, we describe nine installation projects from the past 30 years and explain their didactic purpose, value, and outcome. We select two from the beginning and then focus on seven critical projects between 2012 and 2019. Amongst these projects are a few that we consider as milestones: the feast in the inaugural year of 1990, held at seven locations across the UCL and University of London campuses, where the daring spirit of the event reflected the new Bartlett era. Later, collaborations took place with Sir John Soane's Museum and the Old Royal Naval College in Greenwich, where the complex relationships with heritage and precious fabric were a goldmine for students. In 2016 our installation played a symbolic and practical role in the wider life of our school, taking the form of a procession that transported old models, regarded as central figures or relics, and celebrating the return to our refurbished home, the old Wates House, renamed as 22 Gordon Street. Later, installations were inspired by our field trips to Venice and Rome and a growing ambition to engage with London's real urban fabric and historic texts. Our collaborations with musicians and sound artists have enabled us to look beyond the installed structures towards a major public event and performance. These ephemeral adjustments and interventions can be identified as different ways of transforming a place. Our alumna, Ruth Allan, expresses the impact of this event upon the students' experience and on their five years of architectural education: 'always remind your students that the installation project remains a pivotal and formative experience for life'.[1]

Luck, audacity, and diplomacy have played a huge role in the projects over the years. Initially, the quality and history of the empty buildings we found made them useful locations for radical interventions. Over time, accessibility to such structures became increasingly difficult, a fact that forced us to occupy and temporarily inhabit less exciting but safer public spaces. An accidental encounter in Gordon Square Gardens resulted in a very successful marriage with the Sir John Soane's Museum, giving us access to Pitzhanger Manor and Walpole Park in Ealing and, many years later, to the wonderful world of the architect Nicholas Hawksmoor in his Old Royal Naval College in Greenwich. These unplanned accidents resulted in the changing

1. Ruth Allan in conversation with Frosso Pimenides, February 2016.

fate of the installation's character from large-scale spatial adjustment to more refined, crafted fragments and pieces that embodied students' responses to places of heritage, story, memory, and new imagined worlds.

The purposes of such a group project are manifold: first, to introduce students to the profession and field of architecture through action, not purely observation and design through drawing and modelmaking within the academic studio world. The second is to initiate them to teamwork, confidence, leadership, and collaboration as an antidote to the potentially monastic life of the dedicated architecture student. Dealing with live sites, the interface with the outside world and exposure to public visibility is a major challenge for staff and students, with considerations such as health and safety, budget, real deadlines, fundraising, and operational restrictions. It is an invaluable lesson in diplomacy, leadership, and learning to be courageous and daring yet respectful. For students, installing their fabrications in the public realm is a unique taster of the joys and dramas of an architect's life.

Cultivating the students' imagination and creativity in a structured way comes naturally within this operation. On most occasions, engaging with historic fabric, current life and culture offers an invaluable introduction to the value of heritage but in an inventive and provocative way, which allows students to see the power of the impossible becoming reality. Above all, though, one of the most important purposes of this project is the fact that it initiates students to what 'design research through making' might mean, right at the beginning of their higher education. Research, here, is understanding and finding out how an architect has to achieve their aims by working in a team; experimenting, speculating, exploring, being inquisitive, and investigating various topics almost scientifically. In this project, tutors and students explore together, experimenting in a serious yet playful manner, which makes learning fun, refreshing and joyful. Research is also a constant dialogue between interpreting heritage, history and old stories, and experimenting with unfamiliar fabrications and materials through design. For students, this parallel exploration of thinking and making in a real context becomes the foundation for developing their learning and practice in the years to come. Staff and students collectively immerse themselves in this healthy challenge: it is simultaneously inspirational, fun, difficult, riddled with surprise challenges, rewarding and uplifting. It is a great occasion for bonding and building a precious studio culture.

The six-week undertaking includes the following benefits: looking at and listening to a place, understanding its qualities, ideas and history, and interpreting these so as to develop a clear manifesto. Group collaboration, enabling students and staff to work as partners, is invaluable. They explore in parallel and work together, supporting each other and sharing diverse experiences, backgrounds and expertise. Learning to listen, not only to themselves but others as well, is a key achievement. An alchemy of talents is so important and it is a tutor's role here to bring the best out of all individuals, safeguard and help in a crisis. The installation project is a perfect opportunity for the first-year student to explore what teamwork is about: the alchemy of ideas, personalities and imaginations. It is an opportunity to see the immense value of teamwork, where there is a profound trust between team members, and results are greater than the sum of their individual parts.

The role of making is another critical point, as the brain and hands are the two tools that any architect needs.[2] The project reinforces the importance of understanding the world around us through the tactile qualities of materials, their limitations and potential. Exploring a wide range of crafting techniques with different materials, and learning to dare and take risks is vital to these experiments.

Here, dreaming the impossible is as crucial as realising the possible design. It is a rare opportunity for students, just two months into their architectural education, to work in the real world, whether in a yard, a precious museum, a derelict structure, or a public space in the city. It is a unique moment where learning and practice are interwoven, mimicking a proper design practice where real deadlines matter. Instead of a normal architectural crit, the culmination of the project is a memorable social occasion with public, experts, parents and friends celebrating and sharing the achievements of students and staff.

Research also means discovering unknown facts and stories, interpreting them into a series of designs, a set of temporary installations that adjust spaces. No design is ever fully complete, but the point of discourse with guests, the public and colleagues is to allow mistakes and successes to be equally cherished and analysed.

---

2. This subject, essentially the relationship between practical craft or handwork and abstract theoretical thinking, and once termed the 'division of labour', was for decades a defining concern of English socialist thought. The Labour Party's old (pre-Blair) Clause 4 referred to 'workers by hand and brain', implying an association between handwork and brainwork at least at a collective level. But this concern also arose from and forged an association between architectural and political thought, which was given enormous impetus by John Ruskin, and later William Morris. The most relevant Ruskin text is the chapter 'The Nature of Gothic' in vol. II of *The Stones of Venice* (1849), pp. 180–279 in vol. X (1904) edited by E. T. Cook and Alexander Wedderburn, *The Library Edition of The Works of John Ruskin*, George Allen, 1903–12. Ruskin argues that only Gothic gave individual workers the opportunity to express their individual creativity, in contrast to the pagan-inspired 'slavery' of 'copying' classical ornament. For an examination of these and their relationship to political theory, see Mark Swenarton, *Artisans and Architects: The Ruskinian Tradition in Architectural Thought*, Macmillan, 1989, especially chapter 1 'Ruskin and "The Nature of Gothic"', pp. 1–31, and chapter 3 'The Architectural Theory of William Morris', pp. 61–95.

Here, we describe a selection of installations in more detail:

1. Feasts and derelict sites (1990)

FP: At the beginning, in the early 1990s, the purpose of the installation was to radically question the role of the architect, push to the limit the students' expectations of the course, as well as cultivate their personalities and eccentricities. It was a quest for rediscovering their creativity, suppressed by their secondary education in a lot of cases.

The term 'feast' refers to the final crit, which celebrated completion of the installation for that year. It was more of a spatial adjustment than a transformation of a derelict building or space. The emphasis was more towards atmospheric and experiential qualities, as the project took over seven places across UCL and the University of London's estate. Students, tutors, the public, several distinguished professors, as well as external guests and passers-by were invited.

The banquet itself was a key component of the feast – the food and the drinks, as well as the ritual of serving them – and was designed to be a huge celebration, with a serendipitous but distinguished selection of guests. The primary intention was to question and research the collective value of dining as a cultural phenomenon and to encourage a dialogue amongst strangers. Assumptions about the protocol of the high table, the conventions of entertaining guests, and the set up of the actual table and serving equipment were challenged in surreal ways. The banquet itself was performed in a particular sequence, in seven university spaces. In Senate House's ceremonial chamber guests were seated around the table, which was lined with fresh compacted soil from London's parks, covered with a fresh white linen tablecloth; it was amusing to see all the black-tie-wearing guests sprinkled with mud by the end of the course. The ingredients and decorations referred to London's squares. Following this, we occupied the crypt of the Church of Christ the King in Gordon Square. The layout of the table was semi-circular and the surface was inscribed with recipes and memories from the students' home countries. The spoons were specially cast in The Bartlett workshop, as were the ice cubes in the guests' drinks. We then progressed to the roof terrace of the archaeology building, while the echoes of stories narrated by the students filled the dark space of Gordon Square. Moving slowly through the night, passing through the Wates House studios where a pantomime was performed, we finally ended up in the UCL quadrangle. A variety of spaces were used in the quad, including the undercroft of the big steps and parts

5.5

5.6

5.7

5.8

177

of the cloisters. The event culminated in a live performance in UCL's portico: lights, shadows, projected images, real people and distant views of surrounding London all mingled as a polyphony and mosaic of fragments in the homely-yet-epic scale of the space.

2. Regent's Canal, warehouse (1991)

FP: Our second installation, in 1991, probably represents the most daring example of these projects: we were very generously given a warehouse, which we radically transformed. Wandering in East London, by chance we met a local developer on Kingsland Road who made a deal with us: we take a battered warehouse that he owned for our project and afterwards return it clean for him to develop. Students had to wear steel toe-capped boots and protective hats and gloves, and over a period of a week, a massive operation took place where they were tasked with clearing the space, filling six large skips. This operation required tutors to supervise at all times, but it provided unique training for the future architects in how to deal with a building site, sustain the discipline to clear spaces and importantly to understand and enjoy the material value of a derelict structure. The result was celebrated with a banquet of homemade soups in a room lit by student-welded chandeliers, and culminated in a huge and exquisite tiramisu cake at the end of the evening. The seven installations adjusted various spaces in the warehouse and included a five-metre-high Jamaican hat and a very dark space, where mussels were cooked, alluding to the Sargasso Sea. In the final space, the installation consisted of a very simple gesture: a thousand threads stitched the Victorian floorboards to the exposed roof joists. The result was a delicate forest of red threads, which reflected the robustness as well as the fragility of the old warehouse.

In subsequent years the derelict spaces took on a new character, with crafted objects inserted into them. Most times they were in longstanding private ownerships and were discovered fortuitously around town through accidental encounters, and secured through complex negotiations. We are eternally grateful to the owners that trusted us to experiment – this provided an important boost to students' confidence and pride in their work. Sites of this sort, with their particular qualities, were very much a feature of the time and few, if any, exist now. The merits of the derelict site were multiple: they initiated students into the joys of real site work, risk, sense of efficiency and duty. They learned to operate with care and vigilance, and were able to touch old crumbling stones, fall in love with them, develop passions for real materials and places outside of the virtual world they increasingly encountered in the studio. Those derelict warehouses were lonely yet full of memories, and allowed us to begin a dialogue with wonderful ghosts who inspired our work. On the periphery of urban life, yet embedded in it, we were privileged to temporally convert these spaces into protagonists that hosted memorable events.

The means of adjustment were often ephemeral. Our new components were often found in skips in a fairly rough condition. It was wonderful to see how the character and qualities of the types of spaces that we worked within reinforced the pedagogic programme, with students achieving radical and effective transformations by introducing lighting, colour and occupation, to experience the transformative power of a public performance. Various locations were used, mostly derelict warehouses, ranging from Deptford, Three Mills on the River Lea, Bow, Hampstead Heath, Brick Lane, and finally the Island Gardens rowing club opposite Greenwich.

The second era of installation projects saw us operating within London's public realm of parks, squares, rooftops, riverbanks, street pavements and canal towpaths. We guided our fabrications towards small- and large-scale crafted fragments that were inserted within those areas. The emphasis was naturally on the relationship between the human body and the structures. The sites were in the public domain, where simpler and clearer safety parameters could be established. Fearing that some of the magic of intervening with those forgotten spaces, rich with the ghosts of past stories, would be lost, we sought this sense of history out in our later locations. We inhabited a number of interesting London urban pockets and all sorts of forgotten nooks and crannies. Humble urban spaces were adapted into fascinating locations, where students installed a fragment, a piece of furniture, a component of a structure, or another transformative element. The final celebration or crit was a debate, and was often a race to get things done on time. After two months of intensive effort by the students, the final celebration had a lifespan of a maximum of 12 hours. In the aftermath, each student revisited the site to interpret the event by designing an individual object. The essence of a collective construction and a public event was captured in this small object – like a diary in the form of a model – that had to be highly crafted and personal.

3 & 4. Sir John Soane's Museum and Pitzhanger Manor (2008–14)

FP: In chapter two I described an encounter with a woman who became our guru and supporter for the following eight years: Jane Monaghan, education director of Sir John Soane's Museum. She and her colleague Beth Walker trusted us to work with Soane's buildings and staff, in a collaboration which lasted six years at Pitzhanger Manor in Ealing, Soane's country residence. These projects provided a great escape from the gloom and pollution of central London.

These explorations taught us the value of close reading, studying the particular spaces Soane designed, the context of his life and time, and the culture of that period. Above all, they introduced students and staff to the wonders of collecting objects and fragments from all over the world, and how these became the protagonists of Soane's household. They also drove our projects, as we explored small, ritualised functions to interpret Soane's time, such as the ceremonial opening of the shutters by the housemaid.

Sir John Soane's Museum – a private museum in central London – is a microcosm that offers an insight into the mind of Britain's most original architects. Formerly Soane's house and workplace, it can be considered one of the best sources of inspiration for design research installations. We used the museum, with its rich and seemingly endless array of artefacts, as a curiosity cabinet. In most years, the adjustment of places in Pitzhanger Manor was achieved through unorthodox, highly imaginative, beautifully crafted furniture that had a great impact on the space. It was extraordinary to see how one new fragment inserted into a given historic room radically transformed its character, use and perception, and was always a catalyst for a fun event.

In December 2013, we carried out our final installation at Pitzhanger Manor. The project was given the title of 'Framing Soane' and researched the domestic culture of his household and aspects of his private life. As Soane was fascinated and obsessed with continuous adjustment, so were we as a group. For instance, Soane's domestic spaces were adjusted by the housemaid's activities and seemed to change as she interacted with them. This was achieved via the opening and closing of shutters, lighting of fires, whitening of floors, positioning of mirrors and even dressing the family. We chose to frame this idea in a series of panels inspired by shutters in the Soane residences. Each shutter or panel was designed to represent the action of one of these tasks, in terms of materiality and location of viewing slots and handholds. White muslin was variously treated to refer to the chores: black grate polish to represent the fireplace, reflective varnish for mirrors, and soap for scrubbing. Hinge mechanisms and types of stitching alluded to various tasks and related stories. The panels were ordered chronologically according to the housemaid's daily routine, offering the viewer an experiential relationship with the character and an insight into her service for Soane. When all of the panels were rotated on their hinges (following her command 'shutters: open'), the installation framed the view of the reading room window, emphasising our focus on extension of visual space.

Adrian Forty, a professor at The Bartlett, architectural historian and former student of Reyner Banham, was the only consistent guest and critic of our installations from 1990 until his retirement in 2014. Forty is the first human I met upon arriving at The Bartlett, and although I was initially intimidated by his godly air of ambiguous restraint, he and I had numerous inspirational debates over the years in which he generously shared his knowledge, as well as his extraordinary homemade fruitcake. His rich clarity in debating ideas and great skills in wondering and wandering were invaluable to students and to me. Our brief encounters over tea in the tiny first floor kitchen in the old Wates House, where unexpected debates about students' projects would take place, are among my most beloved memories from the daily routine of being in that building. For our students and me, Forty's shadow and his presence provided a rock of support and inspiration. He often engaged in spontaneous discussions with students about their projects, adding a different layer of historical knowledge and understanding to their endeavours. His commentary provided a vital strand of a university – in the sense of *universal* – education, in adding to the breadth and depth of ideas and knowledge.

Why was Forty's contribution so relevant? He provided a benchmark for all the thematic, pedagogic, and experimental variations though their development. His comments bore out some of the aims of projects, and he always gave unforeseen readings of the fabrications and the locations they transformed, as well as how visitors interacted. He was critical yet profoundly encouraging, and would understand all the phases of a project: the use of a specific historic reference as a starting point and the interpretation of facts by the students, incorporating and experimenting with new ideas and traditional, conventional and personal fabrication techniques. He understood the challenge in collective design research by listening to everybody, but in the end using one key idea as a leading force. He also understood the difficult but unique value and pleasure of adjusting given spaces in the real world.

5.9

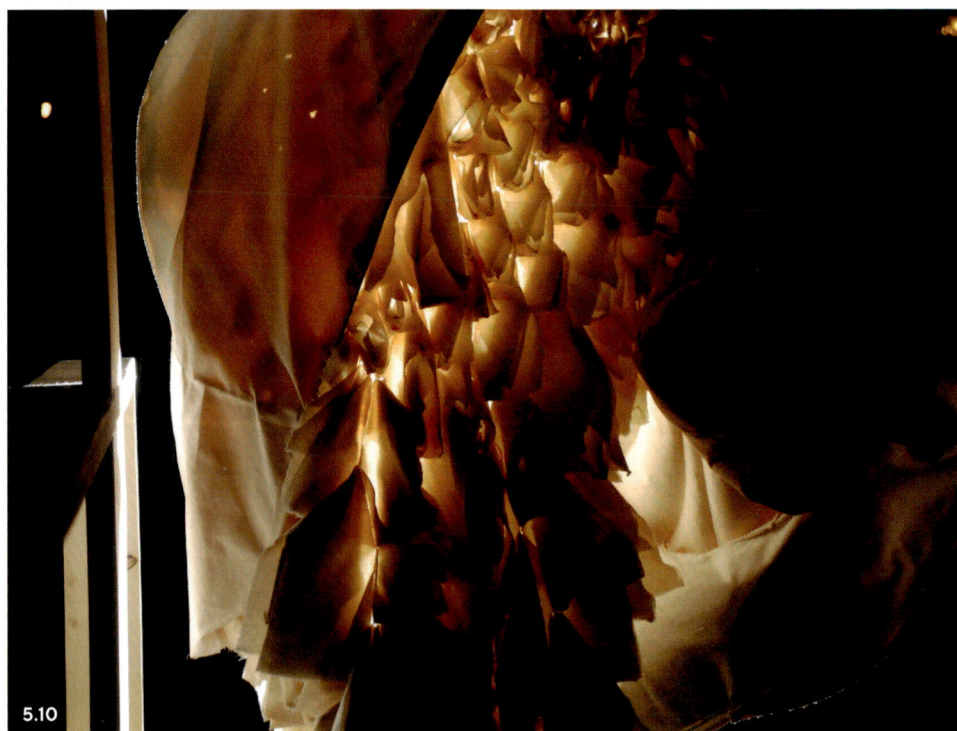

5.10

5.11

Below is Adrian Forty's commentary on the 2012 Soane installation at Pitzhanger Manor, under the title of 'Soane's Six Suitcases'.[3]

A wonderful afternoon, I really enjoyed seeing how you had interpreted the near-impossible brief – and was completely absorbed by the results. In particular I liked the fact that every piece was reliant on so little material substance – that so little had been made to do so much. You interpreted the requirement of portability with great ingenuity.

Card Holder: Very well sited, to catch the last of the afternoon sun. Exquisitely delicate, appropriate to the visiting card, but the structure sufficiently robust to withstand its outdoor situation. The leaving and folding of cards alludes to a code with which we are no longer familiar. And the device itself functions like a kind of semaphore, the meaning of whose signals we are unable to interpret. This is not unlike Soane's architecture, which is similarly coded, full of long-forgotten references, and meanings that escape us.

Temple of Vesta: A device to convey the smoke that rose from the fire tended by the Vestal Virgins. A beautifully sensitive device, superbly well balanced to pick up the slightest current of air. I was perplexed by the absence of any reference to cork, surely one of the most intriguing aspects of the model of the Temple of Vesta: a lightweight material used to simulate a heavy one, yet the appearance so suitable for representing decayed stone, marble or travertine. Yet what the cork models do is to draw attention to the process of transmutation that is so fundamental to classical architecture, of rendering one material as another – and in a sense your installation is also a transmutation, the turning of the fugaciousness of smoke into solids.

Pistol Case: A wonderful enactment of the ritual of the duel, through the unfolding of the device. What was so absorbing as we watched it was the unexpectedness of the final result – there was no way of knowing what would happen next. I thought this device addressed the theme of 'transit' particularly successfully. Not only was the whole work in the unpacking of it, but this process drew attention to the fact that the duel always involved going to some place: travel, and the performance of a ritual. This was a

3. The six suitcases were a cardholder, a model of the Temple of Vesta, a pistol case, a glove, the Sarcophagus of Seti I and an astronomical clock.

piece that could indeed be anywhere, it was fully mobile. The silence of the performance, carefully rehearsed, told the whole story of the device with great clarity.

Glove: I particularly appreciated the location of this piece, and the way it drew attention to what is without doubt the strangest element of the architecture of Pitzhanger, the void above the vestibule. What is a glove without a hand? This device called for the action of a hand, which then reproduced a copy. An intelligent way to make us consider what a glove stands for.

Sarcophagus: This was not so much about the sarcophagus itself as the journey through the museum to reach it, and in particular the prohibition upon touch. So this piece made up for that by introducing simulations of touching things in the room. I wondered whether this installation would have been more effective if the sensations could have been positioned somewhere else, and not in the room to which they related? By creating the devices of window, door, drawer, you had in effect abstracted properties of each that could then be placed elsewhere; and in another place, they would be a surrogate for certain features of the bedroom. It is quite an elaborate and contrived conceit. Could this same approach not have been used to 'bring' to Pitzhanger elements of Lincoln's Inn Fields, thereby fulfilling the requirement of 'transit'?

Astronomical Clock: This was by far the most ambitious device in technical terms, since it involved making a self-acting mechanism. The feature of the astronomical clock is that it gives, simultaneously, various different kinds of time – solar, lunar, etc. Here this was translated into the various rhythms of the movement of Soane, his wife and dog. (Unfortunately, I was not able to hear these). Notwithstanding the technical difficulties, I thought that this was one of the most suggestive pieces, for it raised thoughts about what were the rhythms of the building, of Soane's occupation of it, of our relation to it – and how all this might somehow be represented back to us.[4]

Forty's points bear out some of the aims and assist with reading of the space, which ties in with the purpose of using the Soane Museum set out above.

Our 2013 installation, the last of our eight-year collaboration with Pitzhanger Manor, came under the title 'Framing Soane'. Forty commented:

---

4. Letter from Adrian Forty to the author and your own students, 2012.

5.12

5.13

5.14

5.15

5.16

5.17

5.18

5.19

5.20

5.21

5.22

5.23

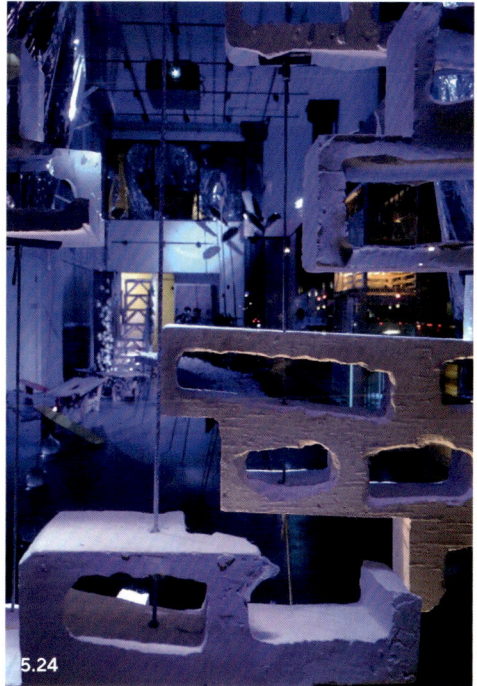
5.24

A wonderful set of installations that revealed all sorts of unexpected surprises about Soane, and the Soane Museum. The constraint of the 'frames' lent itself to so many different solutions, while giving a coherence to the total installation that has not been achieved previously.

The Butler: Emphasised the day/night difference of the Soane Museum. It's quite different by night, and so was this piece. I thought it was a loom at first, but it turned out to be a machine for the capture of endless work. The subject is caught within its delicate web, condemned to eternal polishing.

The Footman: Lots of surprises, a wunderkammer, made to reveal, one at a time, unexpected views and perspectives. Footmen spend a lot of time staring at the backs of things, and of people. Here the footman is fragmented into many different personae, invisible, but active.

The Housemaid: The grinding repetitiveness comes across well. Reminds me of Tinguely's pointless machines that creak and groan through some endless cycle. A nice bit of experimental chemistry with the turmeric dye, and the wax reaction on it.

The Cook: All your invention concentrated in a single, wonderful object! Is it a ham? No. So many purposes, but it resembles nothing. It's always an achievement to make something that bears no relation to anything already existing. The single material (though there are others embedded in it) makes this especially powerful. And beautifully fabricated.

The Coachman: All the delicacy of the coach here, a fragile device that clatters along and through which are seen ever-changing views – the coachman's view the best of all, Soane, the passenger's, framed by the windows, more pictorial.

The Chambermaid: The maid's role becomes a space. This was the most performative piece, that was particularly successful when back-lit, so that the maid enacted her day in silhouette, as she produced a changing environment. With the narrative we were given as the maid opened the screens, this made a nice piece of theatre.[5]

5. Letter from Adrian Forty to the author and year-one students, 2013.

5. Old Royal Naval College (2015)

FP: It was due to the inspirational personality of an individual, then the Conservation Director of the Old Royal Naval College in Greenwich, William Palin, who had also been an education officer at Sir John Soane's Museum, that 100 students were trusted to invade Hawksmoor's buildings and examine his treasures. Our students experienced profound and intimate encounters by fabricating pieces to be installed in unique historic places and locations. This was a once-in-a-lifetime experience for new students to learn to love craft, to explore memories of magical places, and appreciate rare architectural qualities.

In 2015, under the theme of 'Longing and Belonging', two very typical and special locations in London were kept in constant dialogue over the entire duration of the year. The first space was the stretch of land at beach level between the O2 Arena and Greenwich; the second was within the historic location of the Old Royal Naval College, which also housed the six installations. It is the only time that we were trusted to install and use spaces of such historic importance. We were all extremely nervous at the possibility of damaging such historic monuments while carrying out our intensive design and fabrication experiments.

The installation project provided the opportunity to collectively investigate, design for and adjust a number of the private spaces in the Old Royal Naval College, and to establish new ways to occupy the place. One of my most memorable moments was when one of the six spaces given to us, the dome of the chapel, designed by Hawksmoor, was unsealed just for us after years of being unvisited. It felt as if we were entering a surreal place, like the body of an Egyptian mummy, a stomach of a whale, or a magical castle precinct. The trilogy of the dust on the creaking floorboards, the overwhelming timber roof structure, and the intimacy of the distant horizon seen through the tiny windows made this a once-in-a-lifetime experience for staff and students. After we successfully accomplished our tasks, installed all six highly crafted pieces and presented them to the critics, we marvelled at the exquisite interpretations by the students, which avoided damage to the very fragile historic spaces, and above all the triumph of mutual trust between Palin and us. This was a wonderful example of what we might call a community of practice between the students, museum volunteers, security guards, UCL Estates' wonderful van driver whose patience and care was exemplary, workshop staff, museum director and us. It was a real privilege and honour to have experienced it. After six weeks of intense work, we celebrated in the homely darkness of the museum's mews with mulled wine, mince pies, whispers and laughter.

6. Procession and Return: Encore-Playback (2016)

FP: 2016 was a pivotal year in the life and traditions of our school. The specific task this year was to bring the precious year-one models, which we had carefully stored, back to our newly refurbished building in the form of a ceremonial procession. The procession took a year to plan, explore several possibilities, manage safety and risk, and thoroughly consider our options. The relics were transported within five armatures that responded to the needs of our studio culture, memories of the old building, the local environment, urban life, the community, the sky, the human body and specific locations within the new building. The decanting of our collection of fragments, previously held at Wates House, would have been unimaginable without the help, generosity and adaptability of colleagues, who supervised, packed and transported the 120 boxes of objects and models that had been our anchor during the three years in temporary but effective accommodation in Hampstead Road. The repeated packing and unpacking of these items embodied a vision of hope for the future to come.

The name of the project, Re-turn-install, refers to three periods of the school's history, educational life and traditions. The procession started from our temporary home at 140 Hampstead Road with a bonfire of burning models in the courtyard. The following morning, 126 of us picked up the ashes, as well as the relics, and carried them down to Bloomsbury, subsequently installing them on the sixth floor of 22 Gordon Street. That afternoon, seven installation pieces were assembled and presented to visitors: a landscape table; a high chair; a field of suitcases; cabinets; costumes carrying models; a sound-producing seven-metre-high beacon; and operatic voices installed in the main stairwell welcoming us. We called this finale 'Encore-Playback'.

None of these operations, design research, and fabrications would have been possible if the ugly yet humble, generously glorious and versatile backyard at 140 Hampstead Road did not exist. All sorts of events were able to take place there that brought the school community together, and it contributed profoundly to studio culture, as well as providing pockets of personal time for the students. The yard addressed the main lecture space, the school's B-made workshops, the back street, and was overlooked by most studios. It had an uplifting connection to the surrounding horizon and the London sky. The ugly tarmac surface, the simple timber fence, the large steps that formed a generous threshold to the lecture space and the distant views of the close-up London horizon were all conditions and qualities that our school was blessed to possess. It enabled us to design, make and experiment in partnership with our students, and allowed collective spectacles to take place. It was an urban retreat, situated next to the busiest London railway, yet remote and peaceful.

I will never forget the morning in December when our students gathered, ready to load up and commence the procession. The entire school community shared our excitement, as we started to march slowly and steadily towards Euston. Like an umbilical cord, the procession connected our memories with our future dreams. Six groups of students were loaded up with the returning relics. Aligned and ordered, they started that rhythmic walk, 240 shoes marching on the ground. Surpassing any police attention or traffic dangers, we finally arrived at our destination. We were the first inhabitants, ready to conquer the unknown world of our new home. For a moment it felt like a siege of some ramparts somewhere. It was a magical moment of pause and relief, and an opportunity to reflect on the school as an entity, its culture, traditions, and practices. On being greeted by UCL Estates' staff, we filled the empty and pristine ground floor and ceremonially ascended to the top floor with our relics. We slowly re-installed ourselves, and embarked upon lively discussions on design with our former and current school directors, the dean, provost and fellow students. After that epic journey of six weeks, business as usual resumed in the new space.

7. The Bartlett Room G02: City in a Room (2017)

FP: The purpose of this project was to attempt to bring a spectacular piece of urban historical fabric into a room. Analysing the cultural and historic contribution of Spitalfields to London was an eye-opening experience for first-year students, offering an opportunity to explore and understand the historically invaluable role of immigrants in the city. At this site, even more than most London locations, a series of multi-layered events took place that shaped occupation, land ownership, colonialism, and trade. These included the revocation of the Edict of Nantes in 1685, which lifted protection for Huguenots, many of whom subsequently fled to London, notably Spitalfields, and the Russian pogroms in the late 19th and early 20th centuries, which brought an influx of Jewish refugees to the area.

This historic neighbourhood in East London, famous for its weavers' garrets and markets, was both the site for the building design project and

5.25

5.26

the inspiration for the installation. Spitalfields has been home to waves of immigrants from Europe and beyond, who have enriched the character of the area with their skills and cultures. For 'City in a Room' we worked in nine groups, each designing and making an installation inspired by the life of a displaced character from the history of Spitalfields.

Our provocative intention for the installation was to challenge and experiment with various potential uses of the public gallery space at 22 Gordon Street, an intensely used university building.[6] Certain experiments intended to test the possibility of public and community uses overlapping with university activities, due to its prime location in Bloomsbury.

The internal G02 gallery space of 22 Gordon Street is situated at a prominent and exposed corner, yet it is mainly used as a straightforward gallery space. Our intention was to question and research how an empty space could explore notions of density and urban spirit, be a catalyst of various unplanned occupations, and serve UCL, The Bartlett and the surrounding community. We responded by creating a vessel that would demonstrate how nine different approaches to inhabitation could be included simultaneously; illustrating what dense urban living is about. The proposals resulted in providing the occupants with opportunities for unknown events, which were complex and labyrinthine. The day- and night-time conditions of the gallery were explored in their full capacity, establishing radically different connections with the adjacent external context.

The project culminated in students taking over the ground-floor gallery space and transforming it into a vessel that could hold nine displaced fragments of the city, as seen through nine real characters: their history, stories relating to real events and places, habits, personalities, culture, daily routines, and so on. The Spitalfields fabric has a number of key elements that became an inspiration and a reference for the constructed installation pieces. These included the Hawksmoor-designed church, Christ Church Spitalfields, with its exquisite detailing; Spitalfields Market; The Truman Brewery; the Peabody Trust's public housing; the surrounding area of Brick Lane and community; elements of the local Bangladeshi culture; and second-hand shops and stalls. The scale of the installation pieces varied radically to possess the entirety of the two-storey volume of the room, so possible densities of inhabitation were researched and challenged.

---

6. During the professorship of Peter Ahrends (1986–89), he initiated the use of the foyer in Wates House for public lectures and exhibitions under the overall title of Process to Form. With curatorial assistance first from Ricky Burdett and subsequently Jeremy Melvin, the series featured, among others, Richard Rogers, Nicholas Grimshaw, Jacko Moya (of Powell and Moya), Michael Wilford and the engineers Felix Samuely and Partners.

One of the nine interpretations of the brief focused on the ways that Spitalfields was historically a home for immigrant communities. One of the fragments installed in the room was a very long central table. Alluding to the point that a central table is the core of any community or studio culture, it was inhabited and animated at an event where students and guests gathered, shared experiences and tasted all the delicacies from 40 regions around the world. The table had no real surface, and through a very delicate grid of tension threads it held 400 paper parcels, within which all sorts of student-prepared delicacies were embedded. Edward Denison, architectural historian and guest critic, commented:

City in a Room takes you away from The Bartlett and draws you into a phantasmagoric world populated by nine individual installations inspired by nine characters drawn from Spitalfields' long and rich history. Full of wonderful interpretations, the show is a thrilling experience that is testament to the students' passion, enthusiasm and ability, while also making a serious commentary on the vital role of the immigrant in the life and prosperity of our capital. What comes across most forcefully, however, is the exceptional way the students' work combines history and design. Each of the installations is a beautifully considered, articulate and crafted response to the lives of the characters – from a 17th-century Spanish nun to a 21st-century Bangladeshi teenager. The storytelling is exquisite and evident in every weld, wooden joint, paper fold, nut and bolt, wax cast, plaster mould, threaded seam, helium balloon and even candy floss![7]

8. Venice/East London: Islands of Ground and Water (2018)

FP: In 2018–19, the annual installation took place on the Lee Navigation in East London. Students designed and built six temporary installations that adjusted the context of the canal. The project culminated in an event at the community centre Grow in Hackney Wick.

   The site of this project was the River Lea in East London where, under the theme of 'exchange', nine temporary installations explored notions of enclosure across the site. From the outset, the project was informed by connections between London and Venice, ground and water, and drew on topography, geology and urban history. How does water, at an urban and local scale, affect the ways in which people negotiate and inhabit the city? What are the

7. Letter to the author from Edward Denison, 2017.

5.27

5.28

5.29

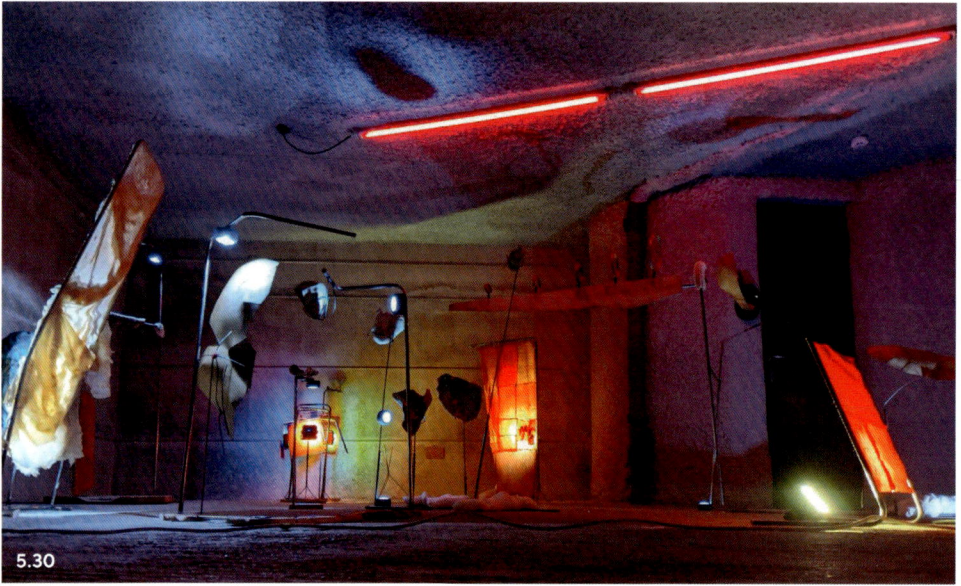

5.30

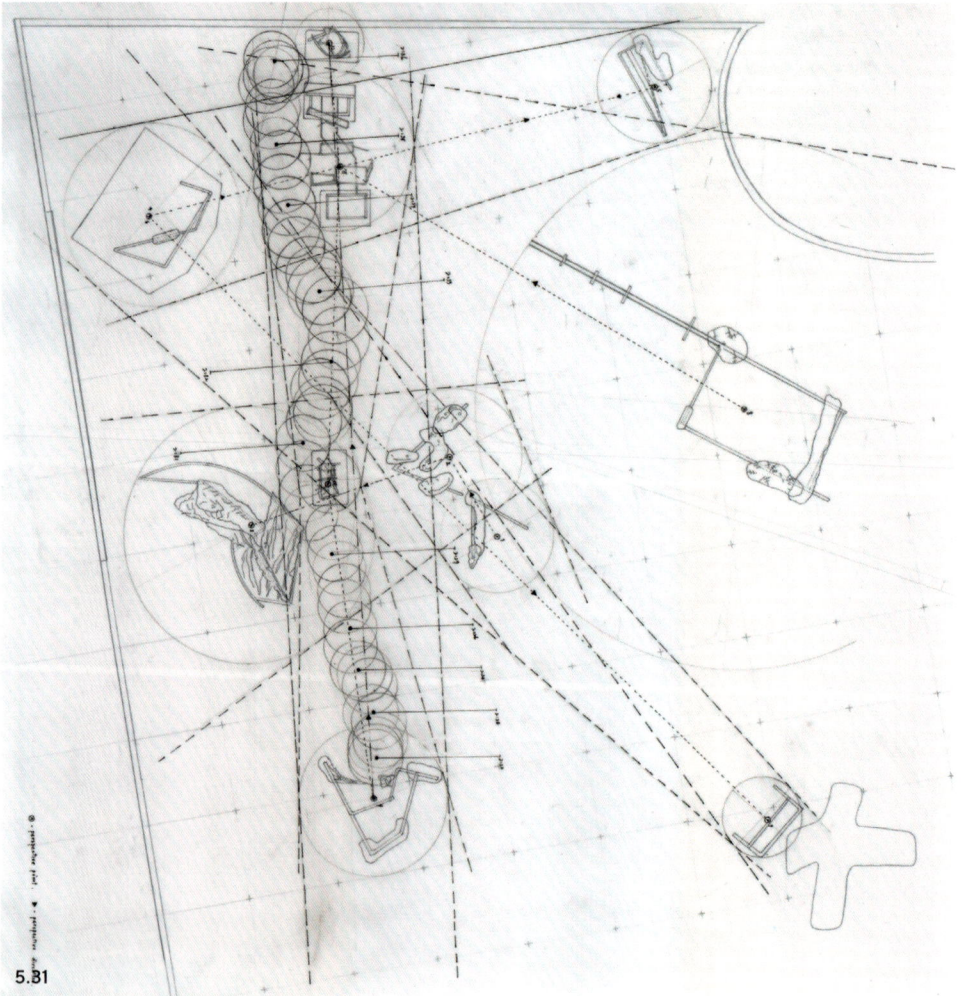

5.81

5.32

5.33

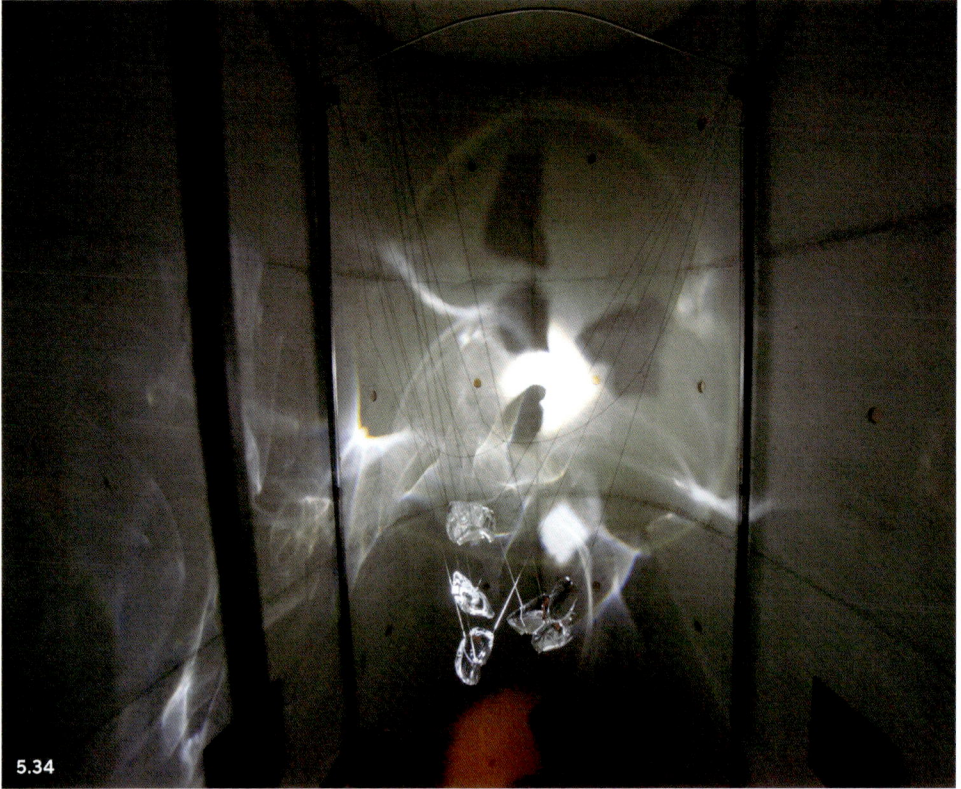

5.34

5.35

connected forms of human occupation, exchange and social activity? What are the physical, atmospheric, seasonal, and light qualities of both cities? How does one's body connect to the ground and the water in the city? What are the edge conditions between ground and water at a variety of scales? What are the various bodies of water in those cities: hidden, still, flowing, tidal and below ground?

The final event at Grow in Hackney Wick was a series of performances in four specific locations adjacent to the Regent's Canal. Seven student groups responded to the challenge. The spirit of that Hackney Wick night in December was a series of interwoven powerful moments and remembered fragments: students' stories while presenting their work; guests' whispers while watching; the sounds of the performing quartet; conversations and accidental encounters with beloved colleagues, parents, and visitors from the local community; floating fragments in the night; pieces of metal, fabric and timber, dramatically lit and apparently wandering in space; constructed icebergs floating in the canal; a red and honey coloured, glowing, latex ceiling; happy faces; echoes of Venetian music; bits of darkness; mulled wine and delicacies specially prepared by the Grow community café; and extracts from Venetian texts. The event was a polyphony of pieces flowing in space, held together by the presence of people, water, music and improvisation. The darkness of that night, the various sounds, the reflected lights, the conversations and the echoes of the music bonded us all together.

Our former director of the school, Professor Philip Tabor, who is now a permanent resident of Venice, sent us a text that was read during the performance of group no. 7, entitled 'Below Venice'. Below is an extract from this text:

We have an old sampierota, a traditional Venetian fishing boat. Just over six metres long, it has a flat bottom and no keel, allowing it to skim over mudflats. We row it, each with a long oar, standing up and facing forward. One oar, at the bow, cantilevers out to the left to propel us forward; the other, at the stern, hangs out to the right to both propel and steer. At first, in the city's labyrinth of canals, we may have to duck to slide under bridges. But once out into the lagoon we can raise the mast and from it hang a painted lugsail.

The subjective effect of the lagoon, under a vast sky, is mostly visual: the swimming colour and light associated with Venetian painting. But when we navigate within the city, silently along canal canyons, between tall palaces, the impact is much more intimate and corporeal. Nobody expresses better

than the art critic Adrian Stokes the emotions, partly subconscious,
roused by the unique architectural character of Venice. He writes:
It... is one thing to walk past a building, another to glide past, to slip slowly
in continuous movement... The hesitancy of water reveals architectural
immobility... On the water, swimming or in a small boat, we are the insects,
the may-flies, buoyant... Our passage discovers the building anew. It follows
that the first character of Venetian building is sheerness and height.

Stokes hints, startlingly, that these cliff-like buildings appear to us as a mother
appears to a very young child: towering above us, with cavernous windows
and doorways piercing her massive skin like orifices or wounds. We swim in
her bloodstream or in amniotic fluid... At some deep psychological level I find
this strange metaphor – Venice as a mother's body – disturbingly convincing.[8]

Four phases of learning

FP: Before sharing the ninth installation, which took place in Walmer Yard,
West London, in December 2019, it might be useful to revisit the four phases
of learning we attempt to facilitate during these collective installation projects:

—   Look patiently, critically, analytically, and imaginatively at a place that
    needs to be adjusted.
—   Interpret the location's qualities and the historic reference points
    – Soane's dwelling, parts of a city, empty warehouses, etc. – as well as
    the project's theme and programme.
—   Individually and collectively brainstorm and design fragments that
    could gradually be synthesised into the proposed design.
—   Fabricate and install the final proposal on site for one night, so as to
    provide the most surprising and effective adjustment to the given
    place. The examination takes the form of a public debate, critique
    and public participation and performance.

In group projects there is often a danger of the individual student being
swamped by the group, their individuality diluted, or drifting away into
hibernation mode and contributing less. In our installation project, team
spirit and ethos, each student's contribution is valued; each member is

8. From letter from Philip Tabor to the author and year-one students, 2018. Quotations from: Adrian Stokes, *Venice: An Aspect of Art* (1945). In Lawrence Gowing, *The Critical Writings of Adrian Stokes* (1978), Thames and Hudson, Vol. 2, pp. 88–89.

indispensable, and it is a matter of duty and care to give their best to the team. Multitasking, interdisciplinary conversations, and diversity of talent and experience are all important in promoting creativity. At the end of year, each student's contribution is assessed individually. Once they become confident and proud of their work, they become self-driven and they learn to love what they do, and slowly leadership qualities are cultivated.

9. Walmer Yard, Metamorphosis (2019)

FP: A lot of exciting events and experiences in life depend on people, places, and accidental encounters. Six years after our collaboration with Sir John Soane's Museum, another accidental encounter with a young architect and curator, Laura Mark, brought us into the magical world of architect and educator Peter Salter's Walmer Yard dwellings, built in 2016. Walmer Yard is a unique cluster of four beautifully crafted buildings, masterfully arranged around a courtyard, where light and water are key protagonists. Under the name of Baylight Foundation, it is managed by Mark, and hosted our December 2019 installation.

Two other encounters, with Dr Jane Gilbert from UCL's department of French and the TOPOS string quartet of young classical music graduates, hailing from the Royal Academy of Music and around Europe, contributed to a trilogy of a unique interdisciplinary collaboration that year. Gilbert, an expert on our chosen theme of Ovid's epic poem, the *Metamorphoses*, inspired and enthused the students to experiment with a multitude of spatial interpretations of the Roman poet's lyrical stories and myths.[9] In parallel to these design and fabrication explorations, the TOPOS quartet was commissioned to compose nine musical pieces that would accompany the nine installations. Their response was inspirational and original, and their ethos was astonishingly similar to that of our architecture students: have an idea, write a piece, try it out and test it numerous times, improvise and adjust, participate, and enjoy the actual experience of performing on site.

While our students were setting up their fabrications, they were enthused by the experimental rehearsals of the four musicians, who were complete strangers to them, and thus a mutual trust gradually developed. Scores and sounds from Ancient Rome, Byzantine and Gregorian chants, Florentine and Sicilian Renaissance pieces and improvised music echoed and reverberated all around the garage and courtyard. As the dark winter's night

9. Ovid, *The Metamorphoses of Ovid*, translated by Rolfe Humphries, Indiana University Press, 1955.

fell upon the ephemeral, magical space, we experienced a deep feeling of catharsis seeing the students relieved after accomplishing a marathon of learning and making. The lonely serenity of Walmer Yard was disturbed; the nine allocated spaces were temporarily and radically transformed for the evening. We felt a deep sense of belonging to a place that allowed us to bond and learn to work with people very different from ourselves.

The group project was based on interpreting, translating and translocating nine parts of the *Metamorphoses*. We were humbled by the generosity of Baylight Foundation, who trusted us to undertake such a risky operation; of course, nothing makes complete sense until it is all installed on site, amended, reconsidered, improvised, adjusted, and tested. After six weeks of hard work, on two chilly winter days spent installing the crafted pieces on site, some wonderful conversations emerged between the place, the themes, the nine installations, the musicians' improvisation and the sound artist Alex DeLittle who worked with one of the groups. Through these collaborations, the students, guests, and staff experienced the true meaning of inhabiting a space.

As we have seen, the purpose of this stage of the education of an architect is to immerse students into the reality, as well as the dream world of ideas, people and places. The spaces in Walmer Yard are far from a blank canvas and already have great character, so students had to explore specific spatial and material qualities that mattered to them. These explorations, together with Ovid's myths, inspired them to adjust Walmer Yard by inserting large pieces that initiated new and challenging relationships for the people inhabiting it. A polyphony of highly prepared and planned parallel performances on site animated the rather remote, solitary, building complex. A huge variety of different architectural elements were prefabricated in the school and subsequently installed on site, which changed the ways one moved around the given spaces, exploring the power of sound, manipulating natural and artificial light, and enabling us to understand and experience new profound spatial qualities and potential.

The usually dark and cold basement parking lot was transformed into a luminous, multi-layered and colourful theatre-in-the-round. It became a vibrant interior performance space, allowing various students' performances to coexist with an endless layering of shadows and, above all, echoes of the music. The damp, quiet yard was filled with extraordinary gigantic luminous umbrellas, and bonded the visitors to the ground through a penetrating rhythmic choral performance.

The dark steel stairwell held a few gigantic pieces of melting ice that very cleverly manipulated material surfaces and magically transformed and animated the space. The skies and the underworld were finally connected with the help of luminous ice, the sound of dripping water, and a highly sophisticated and delicate system of cables supporting them. Another room was knitted into a layered web of homemade threads, creating a forest of shadows, edible cookies made to a Roman recipe, and concrete counterweights translocating the participants into distant, imagined worlds. Up in the yurt space, the truly spiritual experience of watching a short performance, where students rested upon an array of soft and hard 'pillows', with shadows and parallel projections, transported all of us and our numerous guests into unknown and imagined places. The character, density, orientation and occupation of each space was challenged, in the attempt to allow strange Roman myths to dwell, and invited us all to participate on that cold December evening in London.

Chapter 5 images

Many thanks to all the students who contributed to these wonderful collective installation projects. Specific names of students are given alongside more examples of their work in the annual *Bartlett Summer Show Books* and collected together in the *Year 1 Design Anthology*, as it is unfortunately not possible to list them all within the limits of this book. These can be read online for free via Issuu by searching 'Bartlett Year 1 Design Anthology'.

Photographs courtesy of Frosso Pimenides unless otherwise stated.

5.1 'The Dome', a triptych installed within the dome of the chapel at the Old Royal Naval College (ORNC), Greenwich, December 2014. Photo: Jun Chan and Elliot Nash.

5.2 The inaugural installation, 'Feast', December 1990, Senate House high table chamber. White linen tablecloth holds mud, menu and cutlery, designed and produced by students. Guests and hosts: (left) Tom Holdom, Pat O'Sullivan, Peter Cook and (right) Jeremy Melvin, Andy Bryce, James Soane and Chris Lockery.

5.3 & 5.4 Extraordinary spatial transformations (5.4) started within derelict spaces and rubbish-filled buildings, in this case an old warehouse by Regent's Canal in Hackney, 1991.

5.5–5.10 Images taken at Soane's country residence, Pitzhanger Manor, Ealing. Pimenides says: 'We spent several wonderful years collaborating with Soane's Museum and Pitzhanger Manor. The partnership had enormous mutual benefits, we loved working with them, and that opened up new friendships with other institutions. The imagined dream-world of Soane, and the reality of these locations, inspired us all to make great design explorations.'

> **5.5** Inspired by Hogarth's paintings *A Rake's Progress* (1732-34), 'The Prison', part of the installation at Pitzhanger Manor by year-one students, 2009.
>
> **5.6** Inspired by *A Rake's Progress*, 'The Madhouse', part of the installation at Pitzhanger Manor by year-one students, 2009.
>
> **5.7** 'Remaking Soane', installation in the grounds of Pitzhanger Manor by year-one students, 2010. Photo: Bartlett Architecture BSc year-one archive.
>
> **5.8** 'Wardrobe', installation in Pitzhanger Manor stairwell by year-one students, December 2011. Photo: Bartlett Architecture BSc year-one archive.
>
> **5.9** 'The Coachman', installation at Pitzhanger Manor by year-one students, December 2013. Photo: Bartlett Architecture BSc year-one archive.
>
> **5.10** 'The Cook', installation at Pitzhanger Manor by year-one students, December 2013. Photo: Bartlett Architecture BSc year-one archive.

5.11 See 5.1 above. Three acoustic reflectors amplify and redirect sounds from the Greenwich coast, linking three floors of Hawksmoor's chapel to the surrounding land. Photo: Jun Chan.

5.12 'Trilogy' part A: the ritual burning of old models in courtyard of 140 Hampstead Road, 12 December 2016. Still from a video by Indigo Rohrer.

5.13 'Trilogy' part B: the public procession, crossing a very busy Euston Road, 13 December 2016. Still from a video by Indigo Rohrer.

5.14 'Trilogy' part C: re-installing in the new Wates house, 22, Gordon Street, December 2016. Six new pieces of furniture were installed by students in the new building and the first crit in this building took place in the central stairwell. A series of garments were placed in the stairwell, holding relics and artefacts from the past. Still from a video by Indigo Rohrer.

5.15 & 5.16 The departure of the procession from 140 Hampstead Road, 13 December 2016. Photo: Indigo Rohrer.

5.17 'Re-Turn, Re-Install'. Bob Sheil capturing a moment when students present to UCL Provost Michael Arthur, The Bartlett's Dean Alan Penn, Adrian Forty, Peter Cook, other critics and the student body. A landscape of boxes opens up to reveal historic maps of the Euston area, and a series of red heads – weather vanes – interacts with the weather and temperature, installed on the sixth floor of the 22 Gordon Street building. 13 December 2016.

5.18–5.21 The bonfire of models, 140 Hampstead Road, December 2016.

5.22 'Admiral's House', a performative work at the Admiral's House at ORNC, where two people enacted the ritual of making a cup of tea: a sequential negotiation of balance, sightlines, and the flow of tea, 2014. Photo: Bartlett Architecture BSc year-one archive.

5.23 ORNC, December 2014. Pimenides describes the scene: 'With great relief the UCL van has safely delivered all the students' crafted fragments, to be installed in those magical rooms. The work next to the van represents part of the basement of the Admiral's House: these steamed plywood pieces become a threshold that negotiates the world between the inside and outside of a wall.'

5.24 'A City in a Room, a City of Garrets and Markets'. Inspired by the rich history of Spitalfields in East London, this installation by students filled the ground floor gallery at 22 Gordon Street with nine character-specific pieces, December 2017.

5.25 'Islands of Ground and Water'. Installation by students at the Grow community centre in Hackney Wick, London, exploring how the cities of London and Venice relate to water, December 2018. Photo: Bartlett Architecture BSc year-one archive.

5.26–5.35 Ovid's 'Metamorphoses' poems were translated and translocated into nine site-specific temporary performative installations by groups of students, in between and within spaces at Walmer Yard in west London. The setting acted as a theatrical scene for the one-evening event, on 11 December 2019. Images 5.26–5.28, 5.30, 5.32–5.35 courtesy of The Bartlett Architecture year-one archive.

   5.27 'Narcissus': a translation of the myth of Narcissus. A choreography of a performance with three membranes; each transforms and utilises the courtyard through light and reflection.

   5.28 'Phaethon': the journey of descending from the street to the basement is intensified by a plywood strip wall, that is mimicking the existing wall.

   5.29 The TOPOS quartet was given the same brief as the year-one students, and performed their interpretation of the poems amongst the site-specific installations. World premiere, 11 December 2019.

   5.30 'Echo': projection. Shadows and refraction are the visual echoes, and each posture is echoed in the bodies of the performers.

   5.31 'Echo', plan depicting shadows, movement and light, by Andrew Fan, December 2019.

   5.32 'Pygmalion': a series of inviting structures manipulate the position of the body, to both constrain movement and restrict the view, to contemplate the yurt room in Walmer Yard.

   5.33 'Arachnae': a series of handmade webs are suspended by seven Acrow props, designed to swoop at various levels.

   5.34 'Actaeon': a cluster of crystal ice structures is suspended at the top of house A. As they melt, water droplets fall in the narrow void of stairwell, reaching the brass basin underneath.

   5.35 Each posture of Echo is echoed in the bodies of the performers.

Acknowledgements

This book would not have happened without the persuasion and encouragement of Alan Penn and Bob Sheil. I began by collecting and sifting through endless mounds of past speeches, thoughts, notes, photographs, reflections, debates, memories, queries, and experiences related to architectural education and practice. The more I tried to control these ideas, the more they kept multiplying, so the visual material and the text here are only a fraction of the collected and archived stuff connected to diverse experiences, eras, memories and themes.

The next stage in the process was the many invaluable debates and interviews with my co-author Jeremy Melvin, through which we were able to identify that the underlying common ground of this material could be related to three key ideas – people, places, and objects – with the latter holding many weird stories and memories, and allowing us to imagine even more. I am immensely grateful to Jeremy for his phenomenal generosity, wit and patience, as well as his insightful writing. Throughout our discussions it was evident that intuition, and tacit and theoretical knowledge all matter equally.

I cannot thank enough two people who fortunately already knew my work and my personality, and without whom there would be no book: Laura Cherry and Robert Newcombe, both so different, yet so similar in keeping me on track when I needed it, giving me the trust and confidence to persevere, with humour and optimism. Thanks also to Patrick Morrissey and Phoebe Adler. The whole team's patience and precision, flair, care, and the quality of their contributions have been incredible.

My teaching approach and achievements would not be possible, without the generosity, encouragement and support of many people. Firstly, I owe thanks to Peter Cook for inviting me to The Bartlett, for trusting me and allowing me to explore and experiment.

I am immeasurably grateful to every single one of the thousands of students I taught between 1990 and the present day; together, we believed in the power of education, the beauty of collaboration, and questioning what architecture is. Huge thanks are owed to all the wonderful design and media studies tutors from 1990 to the present, whose dedication, team spirit, and love of teaching provided the bonding for our ever-growing year-one architecture family; to our numerous critics, external examiners, the administrative and UCL professional services staff that helped and contributed to year one along the way.

I have tried to mention those who played an important part in the first-year programme since 1990, but to anyone who has inadvertently been omitted, huge apologies.

My educational and architectural philosophy were shaped over the years by the inspiration of Sir Ken Robinson, Simon Sinek, Louis Kahn, Ross Daly, and by the generosity of, and collaboration with, Allen Cunningham, John Hunt, Colin St John Wilson, Dalibor Vesely, Don Genasci, Joseph Rykwert, Alvin Boyarsky, Peter Salter, Peter Sparks, Victoria Thornton, Diogo Burnay, Andreas Kourkoulas, and my family.

I am deeply grateful to my former students Kate Darby, Aoife Considine, Ruth Allan, Nada Tayeb and Elliot Nash, who over the years helped me with their invaluable advice and support, always providing me with inspirational feedback. Thank you to the two recent graduates that were an invaluable team at significant moments. And to my son Uilleac, probably the most ruthless critic and editor, who helped large parts of this book to become what they are now.

Thank you to our legendary security guard Donatus Onyido and to Bim Burton, Abi Abdolwohabi, Niamh Grace, Indigo Rohrer, Roberto Ledda, Kevin Jones and the rest of the school's Facilities and B-made teams past and present, who helped our shows and installations to happen; and to the school's Teaching and Learning, Admissions and Communications teams, especially Emer Girling, Thea Heinz, Chris Cutbush, Stoll Michael, Matthew Bowles, Kim van Poeteren, Amy White, Michelle Lukins Segerström and Izzy Blackburn; and last but not least UCL's Claire Rodgers, Jo Wilby and Denise Long.

Thanks to the caring and inspiring Louisa Hutton, Josep Miàs, Eva Jiřičná, Carme Pinós, Jane Monaghan, Beth Walker, Will Palin, James Willis, Carol Swords and all the wonderful staff of Sir John Soane's Museum, Pitzhanger Manor and the Old Royal Naval College in Greenwich.

I am grateful to the late David Dunster and Pat O'Sullivan, to Provost Michael Arthur, Vice Provost Anthony Smith, Vice Provost Michael Worton, and the UCL Arena Centre for Research-based Education (formerly the Centre for Advanced Learning and Teaching) for their inspirational mentoring. To my year-one mentor and critic Adrian Forty, colleagues Edward Denison, CJ Lim, Níall McLaughlin; Elizabeth Dow, Stephen Gage, Murray Fraser, Jonathan Hill, Peg Rawes, Jane Rendell, Ben Campkin, Nick Tyler, year 1 design associate Gavin Robotham, Sara Shafiei, and Aeli Roberts for their continuous support and contributions to our work. I extend my great gratitude for their invaluable guidance to the deans of our faculty: Christine Hawley, Alan Penn and our current Chair Frédéric Migayrou, and to the directors of the school: Phil Tabor, Iain Borden, Marcos Cruz, and Bob Sheil, for their inspirational mentoring and tireless care.

Thank you to all the past and present Architecture BSc directors and to all our module coordinators. Huge thanks to our past and present departmental tutors and to my first co-director, the great teacher Graeme Sutherland, during the experimental initial years, together with the great team of Gill Scampton, Andy Bryce, the late Mark Hayduk, Chris Lockery, Kate Darby, Stuart Dodd, Fiona Duggan, Aaron Davies, the legendary Jonathan Pile and so many more. Thank you to the dedicated teacher, designer and maker, my co-director Patrick Weber, with whom we slowly built our studio culture. During the same era, we were joined by invaluable colleagues such as Gavin Robotham, Matthew Springett, Brian O'Reilly, Peter Hasdell, Johan Hybschmann, Margaret Bursa, Tim Barwell, Sara Shafiei, Dimitri Argyros, Mary Duggan, Susanne Isa, Renee Searle, Toby Smith, Charlotte Bocci, James O'Leary, Cordula Weisser, Elie Lakin, Nikolas Travasaros, Juliet Quintero, Karl Normanton, Kyle Buchanan, Rhys Cannon, Tomas Stokke, Yen Yen Teh, Mette Ramsgaard Thomsen, Jo Morris and Do Janna Vermeulen; and to Lucy Leonard, a former student, invaluable tutor, and ultimately an associate director in 2018. A profound thank-you to them all!

Deepest gratitude to my wonderful former co-director Nat Chard, who joined us at the transitional and experimental time, when we packed our lives from the old Wates House and moved to our temporary home at Hampstead Road. To Manolis Stavrakakis, our coordinator, and subsequently our associate director; he was a rock of support to students, staff, and the school, during seven years of educational transition, exciting endeavours and finally the return to 22 Gordon Street; for all this I will always be indebted to him. During my year's sabbatical, the enthusiastic, multidisciplinary designer Carlos Jiménez joined Nat. A huge thank-you to all three for keeping the ship afloat and for your support during this time. A great alchemy of new tutors joined us then, including but not limited to Emmanuel Vercruysse (a long-standing mentor to year one), Tamsin Hanke, Joel Cady, Lucy Leonard, Brian O'Reilly, Dimitris Argyros, Stefan Lengen (tutor and later design associate), Emma-Kate Matthews, Umut Yamac, Catrina Stewart, Ifigenia Liangi, Eva Ravnborg, Rebecca Loewen, Nick Westby, Thandi Loewenson, Fred Petersen, Fenella Collingridge, Marcel Rahm, Fergus Knox, Alastair Browning, Zachary Fluker, James Green, Sonia Magdziarz, Farlie Reynolds, Vanessa Lafoy, Samantha Lynch, Alicia Gonzalez-Lafita, Rupert Scott, Graeme Williamson, Jasmin Sohi, Thomas Parker, Colin Smith, Ashley Hinchcliffe, Maria Fulford, Laura Mark; to the Media Studies team: co-ordinator Joel Cady, Elliot Nash, Stefan Lengen, Abigail Ashton, Afra van't Land, Danielle Purkiss, Johanna Just, Agostino Nickl and Jack Hardy. I am grateful for their care and dedication to year-one students.

Last but not least, huge thanks to my current co-director Max Dewdney: an inspiring, devoted educator, a great architect and teacher, and a rare example of trust and loyalty to our entire student cohort and myself. Max kept me sane with endlessly stimulating debates, encouraged me to persevere, and supported me hugely in the last stages of putting together this book.

Publisher
The Bartlett School of Architecture, UCL

Authors
Frosso Pimenides, Jeremy Melvin

Foreword
Alan Penn

Graphic Design
Patrick Morrissey, Unlimited
weareunlimited.co.uk

Copyeditor
Laura Cherry

Proofreader
Phoebe Adler

Editorial Assistant
Robert Newcombe

ISBN 978-1-8383185-3-6

The Bartlett School of Architecture, UCL
22 Gordon Street, London WC1H 0QB
+44(0)20 3108 9646

The Bartlett
School of
Architecture

UCL

THE BARTLETT

Cover image: Will Alsop's studio floor, a room filled with memories and love for people, ideas, places, and buildings. Photo taken at a gathering to celebrate and remember Alsop's life, on 8 June 2018. Photo: Frosso Pimenides.